TENNIS WITH GOD

MY QUEST FOR THE PERFECT GAME AND PEACE WITH MY FATHER

A Memoir

BRIAN COX

BALBOA.PRESS
A DIVISION OF HAY HOUSE

The author of this book is not a licensed medical physician. He does not dispense medical advice, nor does he prescribe the use of any technique, principle or product herein as a substitute for proper and necessary medical care. No one should attempt any of the practices or methods described in this book without expert medical guidance and supervision.

The names of many people, places, and things in this book were changed to protect their privacy but all of the events are true, according to the author's best recollection. Special thanks to my mother Norma, my brother Danny, my sister Jean, my nephew Dana, and Dennis and Jessica Adams, who provided notarized documentation for their real names to be used.

Balboa Press books may be ordered through booksellers or by contacting:

Balboa Press
A Division of Hay House
1663 Liberty Drive
Bloomington, IN 47403
www.balboapress.com
844-682-1282

The author of this book does not dispense medical advice or prescribe the use of any technique as a form of treatment for physical, emotional, or medical problems without the advice of a physician, either directly or indirectly. The intent of the author is only to offer information of a general nature to help you in your quest for emotional and spiritual well-being. In the event you use any of the information in this book for yourself, which is your constitutional right, the author and the publisher assume no responsibility for your actions.

Print information available on the last page.

ISBN: 978-1-4525-6253-7 (sc)
ISBN: 978-1-4525-6255-1 (hc)
ISBN: 978-1-4525-6254-4 (e)

Library of Congress Control Number: 2017907305

Balboa Press rev. date: 06/15/2023

TABLE OF CONTENTS

Acknowledgements...vii

Chapter 1: Tennis in My DNA 1

Chapter 2: Learning the Game in Laos 23

Chapter 3: A Caddyshack Championship.......................38

Chapter 4: Showdown in Bogota.....................................56

Chapter 5: An Unusual Awakening.................................70

Chapter 6: Tennis in the Land of Sheba 80

Chapter 7: The Death of Tennis in North Yemen 93

Chapter 8: Melting Clouds and Choosing a Path 109

Chapter 9: Becoming a Holistic Yogi............................120

Chapter 10: A Jungian Astrologer and an Osteopath.....135

Chapter 11: Message from the Other Side.......................141

Chapter 12: Metaphysics with a Master Healer 152

Chapter 13: Tennis with God..172

Chapter 14: No Malice Intended.......................................190

Chapter 15: Special Times in Mount Shasta....................199

ACKNOWLEDGEMENTS

My heartfelt thanks go out to my family, Setsuko, and the following people and everyone else who helped me and this project with their generous support, ideas, time, energy, and blessings: Bronco; J. Bergley; Allan and Lois Crawford; Dana Flint; Darrell A. Fleury; Patricia Linnea Fleury; Corrine Goellnitz; Dana Hogenson; Cheryl Kumma; Liz Learmont; my Mount Shasta driving buddies, Margie Schwarz and Bonnie; and my dear friends in South America, Mirtha and Guillermo. Also, thanks to all those who stepped onto the tennis courts or up to the Ping-Pong table with me and gave their best!

And of course, a huge shout out to the professional, helpful and patient editors whose assistance I desperately needed to bring the story together: Angela Bellacosa, Rob Bignell, Jasmyne Boswell, Alex Catchings, Consuelo Collier, Katie Dilts, Diana Finch, Martin Grossman, Kristen House, Ella Miltner, Pat Neal (the best river guide on the Olympic Peninsula), and Natalia Tune.

CHAPTER 1

Tennis in My DNA

After nearly 40 years of playing tennis and hundreds of matches, I may not have any major titles to tell you about, but I did have a gratifying and amazing time being the hitting partner of ambassadors, a reclusive guru from the Himalayas, and a quarterfinalist from the French Open. And, even God. An unbelievable claim? You'll have to decide for yourself.

Competing at Wimbledon or at any professional level was never in the realm of possibility for me. I was just a short, skinny kid with a hand-me-down racket. But that didn't stop me from dreaming of how far I could go in the sport and the tremendous amount of fun and glory I would have along that journey.

For most of my life, while playing tennis and table tennis with abundant passion and determination, I was equally driven to explore and understand the mysteries of reality and spirituality. I sought after and studied with several profound teachers from whom I could learn the most advanced knowledge. I wanted to experience and confirm for myself the ancient wisdom and self-realization that people like the yogic sage Patanjali, the Russian mystic Madame Blavatsky, and the spiritual giant Yogananda, and his lineage, were intimately involved with. That type of wisdom resonated with me strongly and I was drawn to it quite naturally.

I began my search for spiritual knowledge in my early teens, but tennis was in my DNA from the very beginning. It is said that we are all made from the dust of the earth. Mine happened to be clay court tennis dust. For you see, two years before I was born in Kenya, my father had been teaching tennis to my older brother on the red-clay courts in Addis Ababa, the capital of Ethiopia. Each weekend they played on the courts that the Italian colonists had left behind, Dad breathed in the microscopic dust particles from the red clay courts that would eventually become part of me.

My early life as a Foreign Service brat may have looked rather charmed from the outside, as my family traveled and lived in exotic locations in Africa, Asia, South America, and the Middle East. My family had first moved to Africa when my father accepted a position with the education programs that the U.S. State Department was operating in countries desperate for American assistance and cooperation.

Yes, I was very privileged in many respects. But as a negative counterweight to the adventure this lifestyle provided, I had to find a way to cope with and survive being raised by a strong-willed father who dominated and controlled my family and me with corrosive and painful abuse.

My father's name was Dan. If I had to pick an actor to portray him, based on similar resemblance and emotional intensity, it would be Daniel Day Lewis in the movie *There Will Be Blood*. Dad was born near Carbondale in Southern Illinois and grew up during the Great Depression of the 1930s. The town was far enough south that most people spoke with a hint of a Southern accent. His father was a coal miner—there were some deep shaft mines on the outskirts of their town, and not much else but lean times and a sweaty boxing gym where my father spent most of his free time.

Boxing was my father's chosen sport. Standing a mere 5'8" and at a trim fighting weight of 132 pounds, he skipped rope daily, ran country roads to develop endurance, and sparred in the ring for hours. When he was in his prime, he hit the speed and heavy bags with blistering combinations and knockout power. He became a four-time Golden Gloves champion and retired with a record of 30 wins and one loss.

While in college after a stint in the U.S. Navy in World War II he married my mother, Norma, from nearby Shawneetown. In graduate school Dad spent time learning tennis by hitting with members of the college team. For him, tennis was a natural crossover from boxing because it required fast footwork and good hand-eye coordination.

Mom got pregnant soon after they married and dropped out of school at Dad's insistence. In no time she was taking care of Danny and Jean, my older brother and sister, and working two jobs to help dad finish his PhD in education.

After their tour in Ethiopia, Dad continued playing tennis with my brother Danny at their next post in the quaint seaside city of Mogadishu, Somalia. When a former U.S. Davis Cup member was visiting the country, Danny took some lessons with him and improved his game even further. But in their newly formed tennis rivalry, Danny was only twelve years old and Dad had the upper hand. All was well in that regard, but the relationship between my mother and father was showing signs of strain. Mom had begun to suffer painful migraine headaches as a result of my father's growing pattern of verbal abuse and cold emotional treatment.

That's when I joined the family. Mom flew to Nairobi, Kenya in 1960 to give birth to me, as there was no decent hospital in Somalia. During this period, Dad instructed her not to show so much love and affection to us children, which ran contrary to her natural inclinations. She sought professional help but the psychiatrist she met with was only interested in introducing her to his friends for extra-marital affairs and so she passed on his advice and continued with the migraine headaches.

After our tour of Somalia was over, our next assignment was to Gbarnga, Liberia. We lived there for one year but Mom felt that living in a single-wide trailer with no curtains next to a swamp infested with seven-step snakes and a local population suffering from leprosy was simply not an acceptable place to raise three children. We lasted only one year there before we received special permission to leave the country earlier than planned.

In 1963 my father accepted an assignment in Saigon, Vietnam and we moved there with him. He was involved with the hamlet counterinsurgency programs that brought American education methods and supplies to children in the villages. I remember Dad walking with us on the weekends to the Cercle Sportif, a fashionable tennis and social club near our house. I watched his matches, looking forward to the day when I would be old enough to join the fun on the courts. No matter how hot and humid the weather was, Dad always wore long white pants so that his skinnier left leg would not be noticed. He didn't know why it was noticeably thinner than the right one, but he never wanted anyone to see a single part of him as weak.

By now, Dad had formed an adequate tennis game overall. His groundstrokes were consistent and his court sense and footwork were improving, but his Achilles heel was his serve. He tossed the ball straight above his head, higher than Maria Sharapova does, and gaped at it with his mouth open as if he was going to swallow it on the way down. Then he sprung upward at it and grunted loudly as he hit the ball as flat and hard as he could. There was very little chance that one of his serves would go in, but whenever one did, it was usually unreturnable. After a few errant first serves stung his doubles partners in the back, they often stood closer to the sideline to avoid getting blasted.

Dad's doubles partners suffered equally on his second serves. He patty-caked the ball over the net without a hint of pace or a slice. The slow, soft bounce set the ball up just right for the player hitting the return. In the interest of self-preservation, his partners at the net often curled up into a defensive pose after his second serves and hoped for the best. There was an unspoken rule in those days that you never retreated from the net unless they lobbed over you, and even then it was shunned.

Saigon spun more out of control each month and nothing signified that more than the time a Buddhist monk set himself on fire to protest how the South Vietnamese government was oppressing the Buddhists. The smell of burning flesh and gasoline drifted throughout the city and into our home as we always had our windows open to catch a breeze. Things escalated further when one morning two Vietnamese pilots diverted from their airborne mission and attacked the presidential palace in retaliation for the government's crackdown on the Buddhists. The palace was two blocks away from our house. After hearing the commotion, Mom rushed me into a downstairs room for safety. The planes strafed the palace and dropped napalm and a 500-pound bomb, but the president escaped unharmed.

Not long after the unsuccessful coup, White House Cable 243 was sent by President John Kennedy to Ambassador Henry Cabot Lodge. This sealed South Vietnamese President Diem's fate and a second coup d'etat took place with tacit approval from the United States. During the ruckus, Danny and a friend left the movie theater downtown to try and make it home. They crawled under tanks that blocked the streets and avoided running gun battles along the way. With faces covered in soot from the dark smoke drifting through the streets, they made it home breathless but safe. Our front yard was littered with empty shell casings. Not long after that the movie theater was bombed by anti-government forces, and a bomb exploded at the American School. Soon after that, armed U.S. military personnel guarded the hallways and pep rallies with M-16 rifles at the ready. Then one of our friends died from injuries from a bomb explosion at one of the floating restaurants on the Saigon River.

My brother was now a teenager with promising athletic talent and had finally beat Dad in two sets of tennis. This hurt my father's ego so much that he never again played tennis with Danny. Dad's discipline was strict to begin with, but over time he became increasingly harsh on Danny. The rhinoceros-hide whip from Africa was Dad's primary instrument for inflicting pain. Mom eventually talked Dad into sending Danny away to a boarding school in Virginia. She felt it was the only way to save him from a possible blowout fight with Dad. The following month we took my brother to Tan Son Nhut airport and he was gone.

My parents, Dan and Norma

Norma's Special Passport, 1958

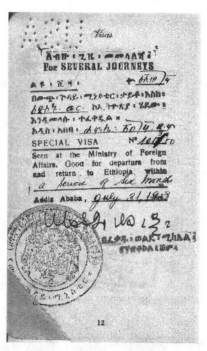

Visa for Ethiopia

Danny with a Greek guard

7

Ethiopian woman carrying water in a gourd

My mother with Ethiopian government staff

Danny and his pet cheetah, Ishie

Jean showing her doll to Ethiopian women

My father on safari with hunting guides

My father with his 300 H&H magnum and a dead lion

My family with hunting trophies in Ethiopia. Wrapped around
Jean and Danny's shoulders is a 16 foot python skin

My father next to an ant hill in Ethiopia (Credit – Norma Johnson)

Jean and Danny at the Great Pyramids and Sphynx, 1958

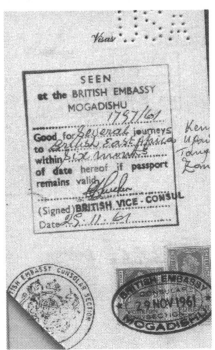

Visa for Somalia

Street scene in Mogadishu, Somalia

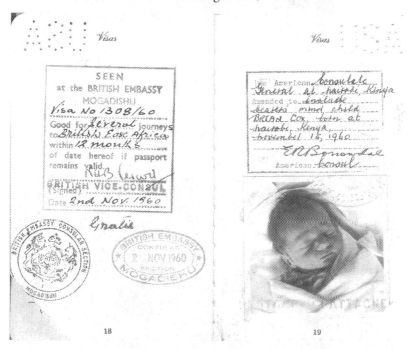

My first photo was my passport photo, 1960

With my brother, sister and nanny Ahma in Somalia

Christmas 1961 in Mogadishu with family guests

With my mother on the beach in Mogadishu

Hanging out with the U.S. ambassador to Liberia's monkey.
I was the only person he would ever play with.

With my grandfather Roy Drake and his pit
bull Butch in Shawneetown, Illinois

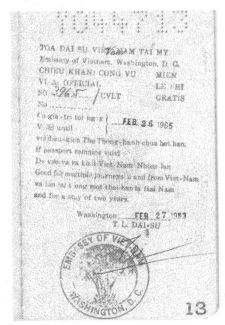

Visa for Vietnam

Entering the U.S. Commissary in Saigon with my mother, 1963

Walking the plank behind Jean onto a Saigon riverboat
with Dad watching, 1964 (Credit – Dan Cox Jr.)

Standing beside a street vendor in Saigon

My membership ID card for the Cercle Sportif club, Saigon

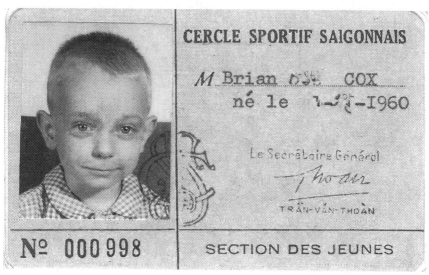

My membership ID card for the Cercle Sportif club, Saigon

On my father's lap at the Cercle Sportif after he
played a match (Credit – Norma Johnson)

At the Cercle Sportif with my mother

With Danny and my mother on a US Navy boat in Saigon, 1964

With U.S. military forces on a US Navy boat on the Saigon River

Standing reluctantly at a checkpoint in Saigon, 1964

Our family evacuating Vietnam at Saigon's Tan Son
Nhut airport, 1965 (Credit – Stan Janowski)

CHAPTER 2

Learning the Game in Laos

Eventually Mom, my sister, and I were evacuated from Saigon with the rest of the other non-essential personnel in the early part of 1965 as the war began to ramp up. We moved into a new development near Taipei, Taiwan, while my father stayed in Saigon. Dad was able to continue playing tennis at the Cercle Sportif and he flew over to visit us every few months. My brother Danny rejoined us in Taipei for his final two years of high school but he chose not to play tennis any longer, focusing on soccer and gymnastics.

My chance to learn tennis finally came when in 1969 we were transferred to a new post in Vientiane, Laos. After arriving we were driven to our bungalow house in Kilometer 6, a small American community surrounded by barbed wire and rice paddies, six kilometers on the outside of Vientiane. There was a bamboo shack on the outside of the armed gate that sold cigarettes, soft drinks in plastic baggies, and freshly cut sugar cane sticks about a foot long. The road was closed at Kilometer 9 because it was not safe to travel on the road beyond that. A communist ammunition cache was blown up nearby during our first night there but I was blissfully asleep from jet lag and wasn't disturbed in the least.

A copy of *National Geographic* magazine and briefing documents had given us a preview of what to expect. It was on its way to being the most heavily bombed nation in history, because the communist Ho Chi Mihn Trail along its border area with Vietnam. Over 40,000 North Vietnamese troops were in the country fighting, and there were over 600,000 displaced Laotian refugees. Every main city along the Mekong River had an airbase involved in the war, but inside the fences of K-6 there were dinner parties and softball games. There was even an American Boy Scout group that I could join. Laos was a mashup of *Apocalypse Now* and the *Wonder Years*.

The majority of Laotians are Buddhists. It was fascinating to watch mornings in the city, which began with young monks in saffron robes carrying their food bowls in single file procession. They walked silently along the roads, receiving alms from the householders. As the monks made their way, the men stood and the women kneeled, presenting each monk with rice or some other food. It is believed that the householders, who are still attached to the physical world of possessions, earn good karma for supporting the monks. In turn the community of monks maintain the Buddhist tradition and share the teachings.

While the monks made their rounds, I began to learn tennis on the two concrete courts at Kilometer 6. At first I served as the ball boy during Dad's doubles matches on the weekends. After a few weeks of that, Dad offered to hit some balls with me after his games had ended. The wooden racket felt very heavy and the grip size on the racket was too big for my hands, but I did the best I could.

"Hold your racket like this," Dad said as he demonstrated the shake-hand grip.

I managed to get a few balls back over the net with some accuracy but little pace. When any of my shots hit the wooden frame instead of the strings, Dad would shout across the net, *"Keep your eye on the ball! Watch it come right into your racket!"* If I hit a ball back to him just beyond his reach, he faked a groan to remind me to get the ball back to him without making him run.

"Get your racket back early," he'd remind me.

After a few months of making contact with other players, my Dad and I learned that one of the older teens at K-6 had taken tennis lessons from Pancho Gonzalez, one of the best players in the world, and he was willing to teach me. Dad arranged for the lessons and I was soon making progress. Those early lessons had a unique ambience; it was common to have pairs of T-28 fighter planes from the Lao Air Force buzz overhead on their training missions.

While stationed in Vientiane, my mother began working for Air America, the airline owned and operated by the CIA during the secret war against the communist forces in Laos. She was the secretary to the station chief at the Wattay Airport. The book and movie *Air America* portrayed the dangers of living and flying in Laos during the secret war there. Some of the pilots and crews never made it back from their heroic missions. But because Mom was sworn to secrecy, we never heard a word about it from her.

By now, my older brother and sister had gone away to college, but they joined us in Laos during their first summer break. My sister Jean didn't play tennis but her boyfriend was on the team at their school in upstate New York and he visited for a few weeks. Dad took him to the courts and was thoroughly impressed with what he saw. Whenever he talked about the guy's "big game," Dad stretched out the word "big" and deepened his voice for extra effect.

"Someday I'll have a big game and beat you," I told my father with youthful enthusiasm.

He scoffed and replied rather coldly, "Shoot. Brian, the only thing you'll ever beat me at is crawling through a hole."

I could feel he meant it. So I headed down to the courts whenever I could talk a friend into playing, and worked towards the day when I would make him eat those unkind words.

There was a manicured, grass tennis court at the U.S. Ambassador's residence in Vientiane. Whenever I passed it, while taking the bus to watch movies or swim at the American Community Association pool, it was empty. *What a shame for a beautiful court like that to not have anyone enjoying it,* I thought to myself. I hoped that someday I would have the chance to play on that court. But for the time being it remained a mirage, far out of reach for my social and athletic capabilities.

Inside the fences at K-6, life was idyllic while the secret war went on all around us. Young girls rode their horses and kids of all ages rode their motorbikes all over a large play field that formed the middle of the compound. The field contained tether ball courts, a playground, a soccer field, and a baseball diamond complete with a backstop. Banana trees and papaya plants heavy with fruit were in almost every yard and some families had gibbon monkeys as pets. For married couples, life in K-6 provided ample room for scandal. Mom told me years later that at a cocktail party at K-6 one night, one of our neighbors asked Mom privately, "Why doesn't Dan ever dance with you? He likes to dance with everyone else."

"Dan heard me mention to someone years ago that he wasn't a very good dancer and, since then, he refuses to dance with me," my mother confided.

"Norma, you should come with us when we go shopping to Udorn," her friend told her with encouragement. "I'll introduce you to some of the pilots. They'll dance with us all night."

Embarrassed, Mom blushed and looked around to make sure no one else was listening. "Oh. You're not going down there for that?"

"Hell yes, Norma—that's exactly what we're going there for," her married friend exclaimed, raising a glass to toast her upcoming conquests.

Wayward husbands who wanted to stray only had to visit one of the infamous gentlemen's clubs, like the White Rose, in downtown Vientiane. Little more than shacks with dirt floors and a bamboo bar in many cases, the clubs were legal but certainly not very gentlemanly. The laws in Laos were permissive in many ways. At the morning market, local women with red stains on their lips from chewing betel nut openly sold potent marijuana that was referred to as "Buddha Bush." Opium dens, which were also legal, were stocked with fresh supplies from the Hmong mountain tribes. Many of the mountain tribespeople were fighting with the United States against the communist forces throughout the country.

In downtown Vientiane, a massive war monument in the main traffic circle honoring the war dead was close to being finished. The local prophecy held that once it was completed, the country would fall to the communists and the war would end. But we would never see it completed. Before the monument was done, we received notice that it was time to pack our bags and move. Dad's new assignment was in Washington, D.C.

On our last day in Laos we walked down the new concrete stairs at the ferry and climbed onto one of the skinny, wooden boats that looked nearly incapable of crossing the wide, muddy Mekong safely. The captain fired up the motor and as we made a final ride across the thick, heavy current. *National Geographic* had described the Mekong as the river of terror and hope, and the crossings at Nongkhai usually brought up both.

With my sister Jean at a Christmas party

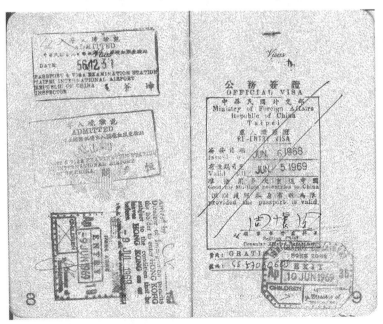

Visa for Taiwan

Stopping to look at local food offerings near Taipei with Stan Janowski

"Brian, stand closer to that water buffalo."

At the Parthenon in Greece, 1969

My father at the Acropolis in Greece

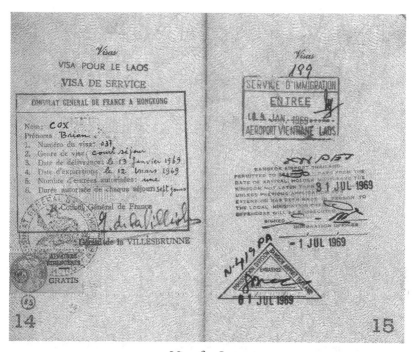

Visa for Laos

Aboard the USS Oriskany, the aircraft carrier that Senator John
McCain served on when he was shot down and captured as a POW

With our pets in Laos, 1969

Jean with village children in Laos, 1969

The bamboo rocket festival in Vientiane, where villagers and other groups would launch homemade, decorated rockets. Some would shoot off target, explode, and nearly kill spectators, 1969

Lift off! Note the brave (foolish?) man on the right side of the scaffolding

Christmas dinner at Kilometer 6 in Laos with friend
Jerry Janowski, 1969 (Credit – Stanley Janowski)

Passing through Tehran, Iran

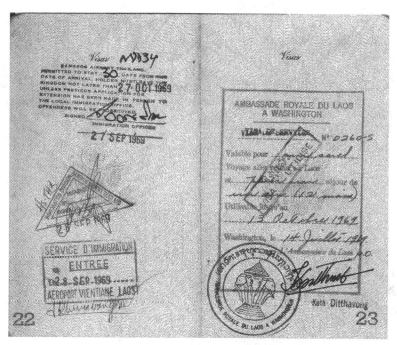

Visa for Laos

Not so Easy Riders! On a motorbike trip to the Nong
Khai ferry dock (Credit – Jean Davis)

On the far right in uniform for a Cub Scout troop hike in the
Mekong Delta through elephant grass taller than we were, 1969

Jean and some friends with an elephant in Laos

At the ferry dock waiting to leave Laos for the last time, 1971

My mother, Norma, on our last ferry ride out of Laos

Chapter 3

A Caddyshack Championship

Once back in the States, Dad settled into a desk job in the bowels of the State Department building in Washington, D.C. He was assigned to the Africa division. But instead of pushing paperwork, Dad longed to be out on safari on the fringes of the Danakil Desert, hunting and sleeping under the stars. Nevertheless, he begrudgingly accepted his new administrative fate. And so we moved into a split-level house in the Virginia suburbs.

My brother moved back in with us that year after leaving college. He gave me an aluminum Yoneyama racket and told me it was stolen from a sporting goods store; I sensed he wasn't lying. The grip was a 4 5/8, far too big for a slight 11-year-old like myself. But because it was from Danny, I treasured it and immediately started using it, hitting balls against the garage door with great enthusiasm.

Despite my small stature, Dad could see that I enjoyed sports and was becoming a good athlete. He had seen me practice on the punching bags in our garage, and noticed how I was progressing with the jump rope. He approached me one day with a serious offer to train me to become a boxer, but it didn't take long for me to respond. I thought boxing was too brutal and bloody, but tennis on the other hand was stylish and sophisticated. I declined his offer. My dream, after all, was to become a tennis player. As far as Dad's dream of me becoming a boxer, he never brought up the subject again, but I could sense his disappointment.

Except for the piano lessons that she foisted upon me, Mom and I were essentially on the same track. When I was 11 years old, I was pleased when she presented me with a brand new pair of white tennis shorts! To me, those shorts signaled my official entrance into the tennis community. Then, out of nowhere, Dad announced that he had signed us up for a tennis membership at the Springfield Golf and Country Club, which could have served as the model for the 1980 movie comedy, *Caddyshack*.

The country club expenditure surprised me because it came from the guy who was now inspecting the garbage can in our kitchen each day to ensure that nobody had wasted any food. At this point, Mom was not allowed to buy any groceries, and we had to eat whatever he bought. The food was healthy, but not always our choice or to our liking. To save money, Dad turned down the heat at night during winter to as low as the furnace would go. He even chastised me for using too much toilet paper. That struck me as rather odd because just a short time ago I was flying all around the world and was taken care of by stewardesses and kind servants. I didn't understand the new level of frugality that Dad was taking us into, but I could see that he expected us to follow his orders without any hint of resistance.

Over time, Dad's interactions with me began to deteriorate. He never abused me physically, like he had done to my brother, but he often cornered me and peppered me with verbal and emotional jabs when he suspected I was straying from his straight-and-narrow path.

"Brian, is this your apple in the garbage?"

"I'm not sure," I answered, but I knew it was mine.

"Look at this, son. Do you see this?" he asked, holding the unfinished core up to me for identification.

"Yes."

"Yes what?" he commanded, obviously irritated.

"Yes, sir. I think that one is mine." I answered.

"There is still some left on the edge here. Who taught you how to eat like this? Boy, there is something wrong with you. Something *really* wrong. Do you know that?" he asked in amazement, as if there *was* something really wrong with me. I didn't think that anything was fundamentally wrong with me, so I stayed silent, frozen in humiliation.

"Are you getting your nose out of joint with me, Buster!?" His face was becoming increasingly red.

"No, sir" I replied very coolly.

In a short time, I learned that the less I said to him about anything the better off I was. This strategy gave him as little as possible to work with. By remaining silent, I kept him from probing deeper into my thoughts with his rather intrusive interrogations.

To avoid him on rainy days, Mom and I would watch classic movies together on the bottom floor of our split-level home, eating popcorn or potato chips with garlic-cream-cheese dip that she blended together into an addictive mixture. Our minds could escape into the movies as we left thoughts of Dad far behind. He hated anything having to do with Hollywood because, in his opinion, it was not authentic, not real life. The only thing he ever watched on television was *Hee Haw*, a show with country music and cornball humor that he related well with. Watching that show took him back to his childhood, which was not an easy one. He had never eaten a good apple in his life until he turned 21 and the U.S. Navy gave him an unblemished one at lunch. His father had always made him eat the bad ones first when they had a box of them to eat over a period of time.

"Life is hard, Brian. Do you know that?" he would say to me quite often, just to get the point across. I never gave him a verbal answer but I shook my head in acknowledgement so that he would be satisfied with some form of response. Sure, I could see that life was hard for some people, but it was an incredible experience for me. *Why couldn't he just let us enjoy life and leave us alone?* My mother's migraine headaches continued, putting her out of commission for days at a time inside a dark bedroom with a cool, damp washcloth over her eyes.

Most of my free days during the summer I biked up to the tennis club to develop my game against anyone who would hit with me. Our membership entitled us access to seven hard courts and an aging single-wide trailer that looked suspiciously like the one we lived in during our time in Liberia.

If no one else showed up for me to hit with, the wooden backboard was always there. The rhythm of the ball hitting a backboard over and over created a hypnotic sound that I loved to hear and move my body with. I found that the best thing to do when hitting against a backboard or a wall was to use balls that have a few games on them and are not so new and bouncy. That way you get a full swing and have time to get into position before the backboard returns the shot. Brand new balls come back way too fast.

By the end of summer, after a few lessons from the weathered teaching pro and hitting with friends at the club, I had established a rudimentary serve and learned to keep score. Now it was time to find a doubles partner for my 12-and-under age group in the annual tournament. I knew I had no chance at singles so I didn't bother to sign up for that draw. In doubles, the best players had connections and were already committed, so I recruited a partner from the 10-and-under group.

It was a risky move to pick someone with so little experience, but he was big for his age and could get most of his serves in. We forged ahead knowing the Sorenson brothers would be the dominant team. We made our way through several rounds and then were outclassed in the final against the two brothers, who had obviously played tennis together since birth. But we made them fight for every point, won a few games, and I promised myself to practice more and do better next year.

To keep active during the winter, and to not have to spend money on furniture, Dad bought a Ping-Pong table and put it in the living room. Mom furnished the rest of the house with her own money, as Dad refused to spend a dime on any of the household necessities. But he and I played Ping-Pong almost nightly using the hard paddles with small rubber pimples that were typically used by recreational players like us.

In a breakthrough in international political relations, the Chinese national table tennis team came to the Washington, D.C. area in 1972 for exhibition matches against some top players from the U.S. national team. It was an important first step toward normalizing relations between these two superpowers and became touted by the press as "Ping-Pong Diplomacy." In his book, *Ping-Pong Diplomacy: The Secret*

History Behind the Game that Changed the World, Nicholas Griffin details the intrigue behind the scenes when Chairman Mao used the sport as part of China's political strategy. The government arrested, tortured, and killed many of its own top players and then in a complete turn of events, later asked the survivors to play against a squad of Americans on the national team.

Dad and I drove out to the Cole Center at the University of Maryland to watch the action. It was amazing to see the best players in the world smashing and spinning balls at ridiculous speeds and distances from the table far beyond what we had ever seen. It impressed me that a member on the U.S. team, 15-year-old Judy Hoarfrost, was only a few years older than me. These were the real life versions of the matches that Tom Hanks' character in the movie *Forrest Gump* played in.

After that, Dad and I went home and began practicing table tennis more frequently, emulating some of the moves we had seen from the top players. I was excited when I received a new paddle as a Christmas gift. It had smooth rubber on it like the ones the professionals used but it was only an inexpensive, recreational paddle. Dad wasn't willing to invest in my game until I proved myself.

A regional table tennis tournament came up in 1974, and I entered the 14-and-under category. One of the younger players we met at the tournament, Sean O'Neill, entered every age and rating level for which he had the time and energy. It was clear that he and his parents were focused on getting him as much tournament play as possible. Each loss discouraged him, but he kept coming back to the table to face every new opponent, match after match.

I ended up winning a few matches, made the semi-finals and earned a very modest USATT rating. I was now obsessed with the game as much as I was tennis. Some of the other players informed us about the table tennis club they were members of and, being immediately interested in improving beyond the neighborhood level, Dad drove us over one night to check it out. We ended up joining and trained with the few players who gathered several nights a week with a professional player and coach from Thailand. Being the youngest players there, Sean and I became regular hitting partners and friends.

We practiced a variety of drills for hours. It was exhilarating to maintain faster, longer, more intense rallies as our skills improved each month.

***

On holidays, we often visited our relatives in Illinois. Mom and her eight brothers and sisters grew up on a farm on the outskirts of Shawneetown and that was our gathering place. Each time we visited it seemed that everything and everyone had stayed pretty much the same. It was our own American Brigadoon.

Shawneetown meant good times and comfort food. There was a swimming hole out at Cave-In-Rock and when we were hungry we stopped by my aunt's house to eat sweet corn tips that were stir-fried with a little bacon fat. Rudy's BBQ was another favorite treat when we were there. The deep-fried Fiddler catfish and hushpuppies at Kilmer's Tavern were Mom's favorites.

The original riverside town of Old Shawneetown a few miles away had a colorful past. In the 1800s, it was a gritty town bustling with gamblers, settlers, Indians, and prostitutes but was abandoned after floodwaters of biblical proportion overran the levy.

Tennis arrived in Shawneetown in 1975 when two courts were built next to the baseball field on the edge of town. I was looking forward to playing on them and one afternoon in the summer when we were visiting, Mom brought up a tempting challenge for me. "Brian, Aunt Sis said that John Logan is the best player in town. She can see if he wants to play you."

The lure of a big win was too much for me to resist and the match with John was arranged. Aunt Sis dropped me off at the courts while running her errands. John arrived on time and was a friendly-looking, somewhat athletic guy. He had short, curly, dark hair and glasses and looked like he was in his mid-40s. We shook hands and introduced ourselves. After warming up I could see that he had more experience and was confident with his game, but I had young legs that could run down just about any shot. So I guess you could say that we were evenly matched.

The only spectators that afternoon were the hundreds of corn plants in the field across the street. With the help of the afternoon breeze they swayed back and forth in unison during each rally like a crowd watching the match. I finally broke his serve, held mine, and the first set belonged to me. It was my first winning set against an adult, and I was thrilled, but Art didn't seem concerned. I liked his laid-back style but didn't want to be fooled into a false sense of security so I kept my focus on winning. The next set I scrambled even harder and, with some youthful hustle, I earned my first title: the unofficial champion of Shawneetown! Nobody knew about it but me and the corn.

That winter my mom's father passed away. She needed to drive from Virginia to Illinois for the funeral but didn't have enough money because she had used up all of her earnings furnishing our house.

I heard her say to Dad in the kitchen, "Dan, I have to go home for Dad's funeral next week and I'm out of money until the end of the month. Can I have five dollars for gas? His response was simply, "No," as if there was no way in hell he was going to help. I never would have expected this level of cold-heartedness, even from him. Our next-door neighbor who had become good friends with Mom, gave her the gas money the next day and off Mom and I went. She drove with tears running down her face while I navigated with a map. It was clear that Dad was not with us anymore. He was against us. And I couldn't understand why.

"Brian," she said to me in all seriousness as we merged onto the freeway, "You need to pull your shoulders back more when you walk. Your posture is getting worse. We might have to get you fitted for a brace."

I couldn't hide the wear and tear of my father's bullying and harshness any longer. He made me feel like I was worthless and didn't matter. The suffering had overtaken me and was pulling me down like a riptide and I couldn't escape. When we returned home after my grandfather's funeral, I came to the sincere conclusion that life wasn't worth going through if it meant living with my father any longer. After a period of honest consideration I made an attempt at killing myself. I had set it up so that it would be up to God, if there actually was one, to decide whether or not I lived. I promised myself that if I lived, I would put up with my father and continue to live no matter how oppressive and hateful he would be. The thought of killing him had bubbled to the surface but I refused to consider it and went ahead with my plan.

I won't go into the specifics, because I do not advocate suicide, but fate or God allowed me to continue living and I walked away from it without any injury. And so, I would now have to keep the personal promise I had made and soldier on.

That year Dad signed up to be a volunteer with an organization that finds mentors for disadvantaged youth. I figured he did this because he could tell I didn't appreciate what he was trying to do for me and there was no one left in our family who wanted to put up with him any longer. When they interviewed Dad, he told them, "Give me the kid who nobody else wants...the one with the most problems." And so they did.

They assigned Dad to a young boy around 11 years old who was bullied at school unmercifully for his appearance, behavior, and medical problems. I think that my old man appreciated being with the young boy because this kid knew that life was often one misery after another. One fight after another. One fail after another. There weren't many people in his boxing corner but Dad was now his cornerman and I joined them when I could.

I did my part to spend time with Dad's new buddy and ended up becoming friends with him. Over the next few years, he and I went camping with Dad and to events sponsored by the organization that brought them together. Having Dad focus on his new friend took some of the heat off of me, and so I liked the new arrangement.

The rest of the next summer I worked on my tennis game at least six hours a day. By doing so, I developed a case of tendonitis in my elbow and a painful knee condition in both legs. Doctors offered to put casts on both my legs to prevent me from doing further damage, but I declined this treatment and accepted that I would have to stop playing sports for a year or two. The only real activity I was allowed to do was play Ping-Pong. In my neighborhood, I was Forrest Gump.

Taking a break from tennis gave me more time for other interests, which included reading books like *Chariots of the Gods,* by Erich von Daniken, as well as learning about the world's mysteries, and the psychic powers of the mind. One day I talked several of my neighborhood friends into trying an experiment with one of the paranormal tricks I had heard about.

One night when one of my friend's parents were gone, several of us had another friend of ours lie on the living room floor. Each of us placed two fingers from each hand under her body while we repeated, "You are as light as a feather and stiff as a board. You are as light as a feather and stiff as a board." We picked up the momentum of the words, increased the rhythm, and when the time felt right we began to lift her. She floated off the ground in such a quick movement that we were startled and scrambled to keep up. It felt like she didn't even weigh 10 pounds and my fingers were not even straining under the weight. She rose with incredible ease until only the tips of our fingers held her above our heads. Stunned by our success, we then let her back down to the floor. We tried this successfully on one more occasion until several of the participants decided things had gone far enough. And so we discontinued our exploration with the paranormal, but I knew I would have to look into the power of the mind and these things further when I got older.

Interestingly enough, that year, trainers from a meditation group came to town and held an introductory talk designed to generate interest and to sign up people for their program. I was curious, so I showed up for one. We were told that this particular style of mantra meditation was the one developed by a guru in India. During the question and answer part of the presentation I asked, "So, how long does a meditation last?"

"About 15 minutes, but it can be increased. Each time will vary a little depending on how it goes," the trainer told us.

"What happens if you lose track of time?" I asked in all honesty. I didn't want to fall out of sync with the timing on the planet, like in those dreams where you wake up too late for the exam you need to pass to move up to the next grade.

A few people nervously laughed as if they also felt my concern about falling out of sync with time. The trainer assured me, "Everyone makes it back in time." Not surprisingly, the Maharishi's method and personalized secret mantras were beyond my teenage financial means, but my interest in the subject remained.

Though we were now living in the States, I frequently kept my eyes and ears open for news about the other countries where we had lived. We still had many friends and their families abroad. Unfortunately the news concerning our old friends and their situations was usually bad, if not horrific. For example, when North Vietnam took South Vietnam in 1975, the government in Laos decided it would be better to accept the inevitable after the American's withdrew, and negotiated the communist takeover of their country. Because of this, the Laotians who worked and fought as allies of the United States were hunted down and killed, with only small resistance groups barely surviving on the run under hellish conditions. The new communist leaders promptly moved into our houses at K-6. Thousands of refugees flooded into Thailand, and many were forcefully repatriated back to Laos under extremely hostile conditions.

I wondered what became of Ohn, our former cook and domestic helper. Ohn spoke fluent French and had such a gentle graciousness, as did most of the Lao people. He had five children and rode his bicycle out to K-6 every day to work for us so that he could provide for them. The new regime would probably have imprisoned or killed him if they found out he had worked for us. The promises of America had fallen short and our friends and allies in Southeast Asia were paying the ultimate price.

***

The annual tennis tournament at our country club came in 1976 at the end of summer. My knees and elbow were feeling better and, after a few months of practice, I was eager to play in the 16-and-under division. Brown coolers filled with powdered lemonade were carted down from the clubhouse. The names of previous tournament winners in each age bracket were immortalized on a plaque in the hallway of the clubhouse. I would have done just about anything to join that list.

That year was my best chance to get my name on the winner's plaque that I would ever get. The young tennis phenomenon from the Willis family, Todd, didn't enter my age group that year, and the news brought me a glimmer of hope. The Willis family had impressive tennis genes. Fred, the older brother, was a tall, swarthy, volatile player. He crushed overhead smashes with so much force that the tennis balls blew through the holes in the fence on the other side of the court (and I'm talking about the small ones that are designed to stop tennis balls). I didn't even want to imagine how bad it would hurt if someone were to suffer a direct hit from one of his overhead slams. Hospitalization, or even amputation, would not be out of the question. A shot to the head would certainly bring an instant, but perhaps merciful death.

I watched Fred play against a barrel-chested man who was the top men's player, and their matches were epic battles. The older man's name was all over the plaque in the clubhouse. On the court, the older man moved like an Aikido grandmaster in a sword fight. He slashed and dashed with precision, flowing from defense to offense with smooth, silent, efficient movements.

As soon as our club's annual tournament bracket was posted on the trailer wall, each of us studied the draw and immediately formulated our predictions of success or failure. Upon seeing the names on the board, I noticed there was one player in my age group who was an unknown. That meant he was probably a real player on a varsity high school team. I made it through the initial rounds unscathed and the unknown player and I met in the finals.

I could always tell during the warm-ups before a tennis match if the other player thought they could beat me or not. Most players usually took one look at me and figured they could win. Most of them were thinking just what I was hoping they would think: *Hmmm…a short, skinny kid with a cheap racket. I got this one, no problem.*

At the time, I was playing with a chewed-up Thomas A. Davis wooden racket that a friend had given to me out of pity, because Dad told me he wasn't going to buy me a new one. He thought I had broken my previous racket on purpose, but it had only slipped out of my hand accidentally during a serve and cracked when it hit the court. He didn't even trust me and was intentionally depriving me of my potential by denying me a new racket that I really did need.

The psychological battle of intimidation in every tennis match begins as each player steps onto the court. Sometimes it is very subtle, but there is usually something to observe in the way each player conducts him or herself. In the particular way they handle their racket or twirl it, the way they loosen up and stretch, the technique they use to pick up balls from the court, and even the way they make small talk or avoid it. In the hidden language of tennis, each tiny action speaks volumes.

As I approached the court, I sensed my opponent's confident attitude by his lack of eye contact and no small talk. While we warmed up, I saw that he didn't look too concerned. He must have been on a varsity team at a nearby high school and was a solid player. But he looked to me like he was just going through the motions, and expecting to win.

In my reality this was like a Grand Slam final and I was the underdog. I had watched Jimmy Connors, Bjorn Borg, Chris Evert, Martina Navratilova, and other great players on television and now the pressure was on me. I returned my opponent's serves carefully and mixed in some table tennis slices, angles, and top spins to run him from side to side. I chased down his shots, got them back with consistency, and barely took the first set. At the beginning of the second set I saw the confidence begin to slip from his face and body language.

No matter how hard he played it was too late for him to fight his way back into the match. Before he could muster any more firepower, it was championship point in my favor. I closed out the match looking as nonchalant as possible and my opponent left the court without shaking hands or making eye contact. I love to beat sore losers. It may have been just a Caddyshack championship but I was proud of the accomplishment. To secure that win with a racket that wouldn't even sell at a second-hand store made the victory even sweeter.

The next Saturday evening I walked across the dance floor in the clubhouse dining room and accepted the trophy while the piano player took his break. Not many looked up from their prime rib dinners or even clapped, but that was fine with me. My immortality was now secure with my name engraved on the tarnished plaque in the clubhouse hallway.

But there was still unfinished business. The only match that mattered now was the one I had to win against Dad. Many a young player looks forward to the day when they can turn the tide and gain an edge over their tennis-playing parent, especially if the parent is one of their main competitors. For many, it is a running battle that takes years, or even decades, to resolve. I didn't want this one to drag out too long, so I kept working on my game and used my growing reservoir of anger towards him as my primary source of motivation and energy.

Every day I was usually the first one on the courts and the last one off. The bottoms of my feet burned from playing over 150 games per day, plus hitting on the backboard when no one else was around. Callouses formed on the balls of my feet from all the running, stopping and skidding I was doing. I virtually ate, breathed, slept, and bled tennis that summer—because not only did I enjoy the sport incredibly, tennis was the only opportunity for me to get back at Dad for all the times he had insulted and abused my family and me. *I'm coming after you, Dad. I'm coming after you with everything I've got.*

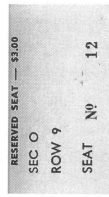

RESERVED SEAT — $3.00

SEC O
ROW 9
SEAT Nº 12

**The United States Table Tennis Association
in Cooperation with the University of Maryland
presents the People's Republic of China
and the United States
in friendly table tennis matches.**

COLE ACTIVITIES BUILDING
MONDAY, APRIL 17, 1972
8:00 p.m.

My ticket stub from the 1972 Ping-Pong Diplomacy table
tennis matches versus the Chinese National Team. These
were the actual matches portrayed in the movie *Forrest
Gump* and inspired me to progress in the sport.

My first tennis taste of tennis glory at age 11. Doubles runner-up!

With Jean and some friends ready for table tennis in our living room, 1973

Playing junior tennis doubles

My first table tennis paddle with smooth rubber, Christmas 1973

Boarding the Nunguni bus with my mother
to go into the heartland of Kenya

With Mom on the bus heading out of Nairobi

CAUTION
YOU ARE LIKELY TO MEET DANGEROUS
WILD ANIMALS ON THIS TRAIL - PLEASE
PROCEED QUIETLY AND WITH CAUTION
YOU PROCEED AT YOUR OWN RISK - THE
NATIONAL PARK ARE NOT RESPONSIBLE
FOR ANY EVENTUALITY

At the Tsavo game park, Kenya (Credit – Norma Johnson)

Waiting to see if the elephants were going to charge us before Dad could
figure out how to get the unfamiliar shift on the rental car into reverse

CHAPTER 4

Showdown in Bogota

"Norma, USAID has a program in Bogota, Colombia, and they offered me a position there," Dad told Mom later that year.

"It would be hard for Brian to miss his senior year here with his friends," she responded.

"State will pay for him to attend a boarding school in Europe, or he can come to South America," Dad said. "Those are the options."

"When do they want us there?" Mom asked him.

"They said I need to be there in April. I can go first and you and Brian can come in June after the school year."

When they broke the news to me, it felt good to be heading overseas again. My mother and I were tied to my father for his financial support but Mom let me know privately that she was going to stay with Dad until I graduated from high school and that this would be her last year in the marriage.

"Do what you need to do, Mom," I told her. "You don't have to stay just for me. I'll be fine."

I knew I would miss my friends in Virginia, but living in America or Europe didn't provide the sense of living on the edge that I was familiar with. Colombia offered a heady mix of danger and pleasure and so I chose Colombia. Colombia had dazzling emeralds, and amazing geography. It also had the longest continuous civil war in Latin American history, with multiple guerilla factions and illegal right-wing paramilitary death squads that hunted them. Kidnapping for profit was practically a national sport in this part of the world, and the drug cartels were beginning their rise to power. A few months later I packed my bags, and I was Colombia bound.

After a week in the towering Tequendama hotel that had a view of the bullfighting ring, we moved up north to stay at the Sutherlin's house, another USAID family, while they were out of the country on home leave. We had known them in Laos. State Department families frequently practiced this type of nomadic hospitality, becoming houseguests to one another until they either couldn't stand each other anymore or became best friends for life. We didn't have many of the latter, as Dad always found reasons to dislike just about everyone for even the smallest perceived slight and had dropped out of touch with most of his previous contacts. One old friend he stayed in touch with diligently, though, was Johnny Walker Red Label. Dad was too thrifty to spend the extra few dollars on Black Label.

"Just enough to steady the hand, but not enough to sway the stance," Dad would jokingly say during our dart matches after dinner. But by the end of most evenings, he usually had enough to sway his stance as he listened to his favorite honky-tonk albums and let his mind drift back in time to his youth.

As we got settled in Bogota, it wasn't long before one of his colleagues at work, found out that Dad was a tennis player.

"Hey, Dan, if you're not doing anything on Sunday, why don't you join us for some doubles? We play in the morning at nine o'clock."

"I'd love to, Wally. Can I bring my son, Brian? He has a nice little game."

"Yes, bring him. We need a fourth this week. Richards is leaving and won't be back for three months."

A time was set, directions were given, and on Sunday after breakfast we headed to the western edge of the city. We turned off the main road and followed Wally's instructions to our destination, and found ourselves in front of two red-clay courts. The courts were surrounded by large shade trees that held a few chirping birds that flitted about. The trees, in combination with the landscape, hid the courts in such a way that when you drove by them, you would never even know they were there.

Ah, red-clay courts; I felt right at home. There were no signs, no country club or tennis shack. There was a kind of sanctity about the place. If tennis were a religion, and it pretty much was to me, this would be the simple church in which I would worship. This kind of tennis vibe, along with the soft breeze, the birds chirping and the sun warming my skin as it broke through the mist, connected me with all that I needed.

An older Colombian man with graying hair approached us and smiled through the fence with his weathered wrinkles and missing teeth. He looked at us through the glazed eyes of a heavy *aguardiente* drinker—or whatever he used to ease the pain in his life—and motioned us to come onto the court. *Aguardiente* is the potent, anise-flavored liquor made from sugar cane that many South Americans favor. This particular gentleman was the court keeper; we never learned his name. Short in stature, he was slightly hunched from the hard knocks he had received in life. He shuffled around the court chalking new lines and spreading fresh clay in torn canvas sneakers that had more games behind them than ahead of them, just like their owner.

Wally arrived and asked the elderly gentleman to hit with me and said, "It's customary to invite him to play. Go ahead and warm up with him, Brian." The court keeper's eyes lit up when we handed him a racket with which to play. Apparently he didn't even own a racket. Tennis players can often be a finicky bunch but the court keeper didn't complain about or even inspect the one we handed to him. His hands reached out and accepted the loaner and he nodded humbly in authentic appreciation. It was fun to watch the joy of tennis he knew from his youth return to him when he practiced with me during the warm-ups.

The court keeper's strokes were as smooth as velvet and perfectly timed. When he hit the ball to me, it arrived on my racket strings as softly as if he had handed it to me on a pillow. After studying my strokes he coached me with some hand movements, showing me how to improve certain shots.

After the warm-up, Wally shared the court keeper's story with us.

"He was the best player in Colombia and beat Pancho Segura when he toured down here."

"La verdad?" Dad asked in Spanish.

"Sí!" Wally responded.

Whatever had happened to the court keeper in life after that went unspoken, and we didn't ask.

We played on many Sundays and every time we went to the red-clay courts, there were no other players there except Wally and this other guy, Marco, who was a Colombian player. It was like having our own private court with very capable opponents. Marco looked to be in his mid-20s, large-framed, about six-feet tall, and weighed a solid 200 pounds. And he had a big game. Wally and Marco teamed up against my old father and I and the matches turned out to be hard-fought but even—they took a few sets and we took a few. After we finished playing, we tipped the court keeper and returned to our rented home in the north end of the city.

At school I formed a friendship with another American newcomer, Paul Fowler. His father worked for the U.S. Naval Forces in Colombia. Paul had a big tennis game as well. He and his brother and father played "power tennis." They had wicked kick serves that jumped up to shoulder level, sizzling flat backhands that zipped a quarter-inch above the net, and deadly accurate forehands. Paul's father played with an unlit cigar in his mouth, which added to his larger-than-life presence on the court.

They played at a private club where the ball boys throw you two balls at once from across the court. The balls land one after another in perfect sequence so you can catch them one at a time. I enjoy throwing balls using that method to people who have not seen it before, watching the confused receiver having to adjust to two incoming objects. They usually fumble the catch.

The high school we attended was perched on a steep slope with a view of Bogota. Two macadam tennis courts were terraced onto the side of a ridge and were surrounded by eucalyptus trees with dry leaves that chattered in the wind. The courts were higher in altitude than Machu Picchu, Peru, so they might be some of the highest in the world. At this elevation, we had to use pressure-less balls, and they take some getting used to because they feel rather hard. We tried hitting with some regular ones, but they bounced as if we were playing on the moon.

I was 16 years old now, was taking more games off my old man in tennis, but had not yet beaten him in a full set. One Saturday morning on the courts at my school, we got ready to play singles against each other. Bjorn Borg was my idol at the time and so it was my silent, stoic Borg against Dad's fiery, tempestuous Jimmy Connors. The ritual began with a brief warm up to get the joints moving and to find the right timing, a few practice serves, then the spinning of the racket handle up or down to see who served. "I'll serve first," I said to him after winning the call.

Each of us began the first game with more than the usual focus. Our matches up to this point were very close and he knew I was gaining on him. There was no talking or joking. I fired up every bit of motivation I could but kept on a poker face so that Dad wouldn't see how much this match really meant if I could only win it. My serves were landing with good placement but not as much pop as I wanted. I was still using the old, chewed-up Thomas A. Davis racket with a thin neck and it badly needed re-stringing. It looked and played more like a badminton racket so I had to exert extra effort. I used some head fakes when approaching the net and cut off Dad's angles. I held serve, then broke his—*ding!* And so the first two games went to the young challenger. *Gentlemen, to your corners!*

At the start of the third game I played even more aggressively to let him know I wasn't going to back off. This was no time to show mercy and he deserved none. I held serve and pulled further ahead. He fought back, but he couldn't raise his game any further. The first set ended in my favor. The second set followed the same pattern and the match was soon mine. I didn't care if there were any trophies involved—his misery was my trophy and this was the most satisfying win of my life. I was ready for more set but he motioned to me and said, "That's all for today, Brian. Let's go."

As we gathered our equipment and walked to the car, there was no friendly, "Congratulations, Brian. You played really well. I'm proud that you finally beat me. Let's see if you can do it again next time," or anything like that.

Dad's mood was subdued after the game, and we didn't speak on the drive home. I almost felt a twinge of sorrow for the son of a bitch but quickly reminded myself of all the hurt he caused us and was still dishing out on a regular basis. That day was the last time we played against each other in singles. The prospect of losing to me for the rest of his life must have been more than he could face, so he never again asked me to play against him. However, we continued playing doubles as partners on the weekends with Wally, Marco, and the old Colombian court keeper.

I practiced a few times with Paul to prepare for the tryout matches that would determine the rankings for our school team. After seeing his game, I was sure that he would be the number-one player on the team, but I had yet to see one of the Colombian's play. When I finally saw his game, I was in awe. He played with an extremely high level of grace and natural ability. Miguel Cortez surprised me by beating Paul and taking the number-one spot.

I thought I had the number-three spot locked up, but that was just wishful thinking. In one match I played a sophomore who had some basic strokes but nothing too fancy. Though my outfit and shots looked classier and I had spent more time on my game than he had, it didn't seem to matter; the dude was a human backboard and kept blocking my shots back with little regard to style. I soon became frustrated and the more upset I became, the faster the match slipped through my fingers. I was forced to swallow my pride with that loss.

One of the adventures of playing in Colombia was the team trip to Medellin. We would have driven there but anti-government rebels sprang out of the jungles along the way, kidnapped people, and kept them in captivity for years. Army and police roadblocks were set up at certain positions along the way, but they couldn't control the entire distance. So as a precaution we bought tickets for the flight.

We strutted out to the tarmac with our rackets and carry-on bags past the armed guards, and then walked up the mobile ramp that took us into the plane. The familiar roar of the engines was with me once again and we were soon soaring above the clouds. We eventually circled over the lush hillsides of Medellin and landed. We were now in the hometown of Pablo Escobar, the notorious drug cartel leader that would soon bring the country to its knees.

The next morning at the courts, Paul walked over to where I was standing. "I think I might have food poisoning," he said.

"Yeah," I said to him. "You look really pale. Do you want some water?"

"No. I just drank some orange juice. Let's go warm up." Then he hesitated, leaned over some bushes, and threw up. This was not a good omen, as we were paired for number-one doubles. But even in his weakened state, Paul was strong enough to make it through the early rounds, and together we were beating school teams from all across the country. We made it to the finals of the tournament the next day.

The games were agonizingly close. We were even in sets against Colombia's national junior champions and were just a couple of games away from what would possibly be a huge tennis win—the kind that I could fondly replay in my mind for years to come. But when a few points got away from us, the Colombians watching the match from outside of the fence gathered and cheered louder for their countrymen. I looked over at my partner and he was running out of energy with each step. He was sweaty and pale and looked like he was going to pass out. *Hang in there, buddy. We can do this!*

At advantage out, match point against us, I felt there was still hope. Paul placed a kick serve to the ad court. Our opponent stepped into the ball with a strong lefty forehand and drilled it right at my midsection. I reacted as fast as I could—but the ball nicked the throat of my racket and dropped into the net, taking my heart along with it. The partisan crowd immediately erupted in cheers for their fellow Colombians and we shook hands at the net with our opponents. *Game, set, crap. Dammit, Dad! If you had given me a decent racket we could have won that match.* We took Paul to get him some rest and whatever medicine he needed. But there was a consolation for us that year. Our team, along with the women's team, swept the city high school championships in Bogota undefeated.

On many evenings, Dad asked me, "What's your plan tonight? Want to go downtown to play some table tennis?" Fortunately, I had already established my dominance over him in table tennis, and he had adjusted to this.

If I didn't have other plans I always responded with, "What time does the bus leave?"

"Right after dinner."

"Sounds good."

We left the house soon after eating and headed south along Septima Street, a main thoroughfare in Bogota. Then we turned right on the Avenue of the Americas. The table tennis parlors were located close to the city center. They consisted of several floors of rooms filled with rows of sturdy wooden tables, crowded with Colombians who gathered to socialize, smoke cigarettes, drink beer, and hang out long into the night. When Dad and I showed up with his custom Butterfly paddles and Nittaku three-star, premium, optic, yellow balls, we became an instant attraction. A few of the better and most curious Colombian players always approached us and could hardly wait to test their skills against the only gringos there.

At those Bogota table tennis parlors, we faced off in doubles against their best players. Dad was the steady setup man and I was the hammer who finished off points with no mercy. The games grew increasingly fun as the nights went on, as everyone became better able to anticipate each other's shots. Better teams formed to take us on as word spread throughout the clubs that some good action was happening. With Dad's exaggerated facial expressions and good-natured jabbering in basic Spanish, those nights in Bogota were some of the best times we shared. And through it all, we never lost a match. When we were playing and winning like this, Dad was too busy having fun to find problems with me and those nights in Bogota became precious moments.

Although Mom wanted to stay in Colombia until my school year ended, her situation with Dad took a turn for the worse one evening when I was away. She had gone bowling at with some friends and when she returned the deadbolts on the house were locked from the inside, and she didn't have her keys for them. After ringing the doorbell and knocking on the windows, Dad never showed up so she went across the street and was able to stay with neighbors she had never met.

The next morning Mom knocked on the door at our house, but again there was no answer. She climbed over the back fence and peered through the window to their bedroom to see Dad putting on his clothes for work. She knocked on the window and he gave her an irritated glance. Then he walked to the back door and unlocked it for her.

"Why didn't you let me in last night, Dan? Didn't you hear me knocking?" She shoved him on the chest to show her frustration. Then he slapped her hard across the face. It shocked her, but that was all the motivation she needed to finally decide to leave him. He glared at her in silence and she walked away from him to avoid being hit again. While taking a shower after the confrontation, Mom found several long red hairs in her shower cap, and that's when she knew why Dad had locked her out. Mom didn't have red hair.

Mom soon let me know that she was finally leaving Dad for good, and then departed for Oregon in pursuit of a divorce and a new start. She was 54 years old, and had little money or self-esteem after living with Dad for so many years. She really didn't know if she could make it on her own but this time she felt she had no choice but to try. We hugged and I kissed her cheek before she said goodbye and got into a taxi to the airport. She had escaped her captivity after 30 years of marriage.

***

At the end of the school year Paul swung by our house unexpectedly one night. I figured it might be to head out for some three-on-three basketball in the parks with another one of our friends who played on the junior varsity team.

"Hey! Come on in. How's it going?" I asked."

"Not good," he said with a serious tone. We've been given notice to leave the country within 48 hours. I have to leave for California on Saturday."

"What happened?" I asked.

"We were notified that the drug lords have us on their death list."

"That doesn't sound good. Was anyone following you on the way over?"

"No, I double-backed at Unicentro to make sure."

We talked for a few more minutes and Paul said, "Let's keep in touch, and we'll get together when you get back to the States."

"Let's do that."

After graduation, I spent my last four nights in Bogota visiting a German girl that I had been dating. On our last evening together we visited a site overlooking the city center and I wondered if we would ever see each other again. Given our young ages, the chances were slim.

"Please don't forget me," she said.

"I won't, Edith. I won't." We put our foreheads together and shared a sad kiss before I took her home.

The next morning I shook hands with Dad after he gave me a ride to the airport. I was headed back to the States to begin college. His final words of advice for me were, "Brian, you need to massage your scalp more. Your hair needs more body like mine." And he said this with serious intent. My hair was blonde, straight and very fine, very unlike his dark, wavy hair and he thought that massaging my scalp could turn things around for me.

"Yes, sir, I will," I told him, even though the last thing I would ever want would be to look more like him.

I headed toward the boarding gate and I was finally free from Dad, —or so I thought. I was unaware that the emotional and psychological wounds I had received from him were now buried deep within me.

My Official Passport

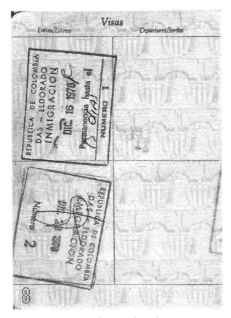

Visas for Colombia

Visa for Costa Rica

With Dad in Costa Rica

Playing table tennis with Dad in Costa Rica

Can't you just feel the holiday cheer? Christmas dinner 1978
in Bogota with my grandfather, mother and father

With my grandparents, Oscar and Lena Cox, at our house in Bogota

My grandparents in the mountains near Bogota

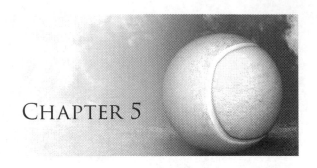

CHAPTER 5

An Unusual Awakening

I relocated to the Pacific Northwest for college, mainly because my sister lived there. I moved into the dorm on the fifth floor of a notoriously rowdy all-men's floor. The dorm had two outdoor tennis courts just an elevator ride away from my room.

In classes and at social functions I met a few members of the tennis team. Based on my bravado and seeing me hit on the courts outside the dorm, they encouraged me to show up as a walk-on for the upcoming team tryouts. The university had an NCAA Division I team. I figured I had nothing to lose so I went to see what I could do. Fortunately, I had recently switched from the lowly hand-me-down wooden racket to an aluminum Yonex and I was very happy with that upgrade. My old man had finally come through for me, and I had received the racket as a Christmas gift.

At the tryouts we played some doubles and singles against the other players with the coach watching. A few days later the roster was posted. To my surprise, my name was on it! The Pac-10 had won about two-thirds of the Division I championships. My old man would finally have to acknowledge that I had a big game. I mentioned making the team to him in a letter but he never brought it up in his reply. He was never big on compliments.

After a few nights of hitching rides to practices at a tennis center where the cheap motels and prostitutes on the road outside outnumbered the tennis players—the glamour of being on the team quickly wore off. There was no scholarship in it for me and I was just not a late-night player. I also realized the amount of commitment and energy it was going to take, and decided I didn't want to sacrifice my education, my sleep, or my social life. The most important thing for me in tennis was playing for the pure enjoyment of the game, when and with whomever I wanted. I also gave up trying to prove myself to my father, and this took a tremendous amount of weight off my shoulders.

But I was still a late-night table tennis player and was not willing to give that up. There was a table in the basement of one of the other dorms, and Steve Thomas and I went over to check it out. We found the table to be available with adequate space to play. The way his shots were going he had obviously played before. He began to keep up with the shots I was feeding him and followed the drill as if we were in a training session at the table tennis club in Virginia. Before long we were hitting at higher speeds further back from the table and still maintaining good control. Each rally went for longer periods of time than the previous ones. We were amazingly in sync with the timing and action of each shot, in a way I had never fully experienced for that length of time. During the session we definitely entered into some form of a unified flow. As we began to lose concentration, we began to miss more shots and the magic of the previous moments ended. We took a break to cool down.

"This is so amazing—I've never played this well before!" exclaimed my hitting partner.

Wiping the sweat from my forehead, I agreed. "Yeah, some of those rallies were incredible."

"That was amazing! Our shots just kept going in."

"Yeah, we were in the zone, for sure."

"We need to play more often," he said, as we packed up our gear and left.

Marty Reisman, the famous table tennis champion and hustler of big money games said in a documentary interview at the end of his career that he was familiar with working himself up into state of hypnosis when he played that made him feel like he was floating on air in a state of near euphoria. My hitting partner and I had slipped into that state and stayed in it deeply for what felt like 10 minutes or so and it was absolutely wonderful.

***

Another dorm neighbor and new friend of mine, Nathaniel, shared some of his mystical books and Eastern philosophical ideas with me. One book he loaned me was *The Secret of the Andes,* and I soon began to read more about spiritually advanced masters who knew the wisdom of the East. To pursue things further, I also took a course in comparative religions one quarter, and was able to formally study different traditions and texts. I saw value in all of them, but I was especially drawn to the *Tao Te Ching* and other classic texts composed from Eastern perspectives.

Nate told me one day that there was a Victorian-style mansion on Capitol Hill down the road from the cemetery where Bruce Lee is buried. It housed a group called the Aquarian Foundation. The leader claimed to be in contact with a group of advanced beings that included an assortment of ascended masters, some of whom were the same ones said to have been in contact with Madame Blavatsky in the late 1800s. This sounded like fun to me, so I poked my head into the old house one afternoon.

The place was headed by a psychic-medium named Keith Milton Rhinehart, who claimed to be afflicted with the stigmata of Jesus and performed healing miracles. So I checked out the schedule, attended a meeting one night, and listened to a brief lecture from one of their speakers. A photo album in the lobby revealed pictures of psychic surgeries performed with the hands and no instruments. The concept and photos were so unusual that I didn't really know if they were real or not. Rhinehart remained elusive, and I never visited the center again.

With a growing aspiration toward something spiritual that I couldn't quite define, but perhaps could be termed as "enlightenment," one evening in my dorm room I sat down in a meditative posture and began to focus my concentration on reaching such a state of consciousness. It took Buddha forty days of constant meditation to get there and I was demanding it immediately. *If the Eastern Masters can do it, so can I*, I thought.

Focusing myself on that lofty goal, I felt as if all of my highest thoughts and feelings fused with an intense desire for a higher or more complete state of expanded consciousness.

And so I sat quietly in a comfortable chair and let the process continue. Engaged in this activity second by second, minute by minute, I lost track of time. After what could have been an hour, I found that the flow of energy was not nearly as strong as when I started the session. This mysterious energy I'd been exerting tapered off until I had nothing left to give; I was an empty vessel. On a subtle level, there was a total void of life-force emanating from me or to me—I felt totally alone and cut off from the source of energy with which I'd previously been provided. If there is such a thing as "the dark night of the soul," this sure felt like it.

Opening my eyes slowly in the darkness of my room, I perceived a very faint light around me that extended visibly just beyond me. I moved very slowly to watch the interaction of my breath, my thoughts, and my awareness in association with this subtle light. The energy that was released within my body during whatever process I had just undergone was more than my body was ready to handle, like some form of electrical overload. I wasn't sure if I was going to survive the night given the intensity of the incident and I wondered if my body was going to be burnt to a crisp, as I was now exhausted and couldn't stay awake any longer. My last thought before I drifted off to sleep was that, if tomorrow came and I was still intact, things would be very different.

The next morning, to my surprise, I woke up and saw that my body was still intact and functioning. I noticed that my mind was just observing things and not formulating any specific words or thoughts. There was a deep silence and calm within my mind. I pulled myself together and got dressed, because I had to head out for classes. As I interacted with other people and the rest of the world outside my dorm room, my way of relating to the world appeared to have changed. I felt like a different person. I was enjoying this new state of not having to create any thoughts or emotions at all while still being able to function in the outside world.

There was also a refreshing pleasure of interacting with whatever was going on, and a renewed enjoyment of being alive. With this new way of being, as I ate each piece of food in the cafeteria, I experienced the tastes and textures as if I was ingesting food for the first time. My preconceived ideas about anything having to taste or be a certain way to please me were completely gone. I seemed to be accepting everything as it was without attaching a thought or emotional reaction to it. I also had a strong desire to be more authentic to others and to myself in each moment. Suddenly, I no longer needed to say certain things to people out of any social or cultural expectation.

One evening when a group of friends and I sat in my next-door neighbor's room, instead of engaging in my normal "personality" mode, directing the conversation in some way or another as I would have in the past, to gain attention perhaps, I kept more quiet and allowed others to express themselves and share their thoughts and ideas more freely. While practicing this more conscious way of interacting with those in the room, I saw a subtle light around their bodies that expanded and glowed brighter when they were enthused and doing the talking. I noticed that whenever my input controlled or steered the conversation to something I was trying to get attention with, this shut out the opportunity for others to literally open up and shine *their* light.

Observing my own perceptions of reality had always been fascinating for me, but I now had a much more precise awareness of my own presence and its impact on people and things around me. Each breath I took and every thought, motive, and personal agenda that came up within me was magnified for my immediate inspection. It was both excruciating and exhilarating to be so aware.

The third night after the unusual transformation, I was on my bed with my eyes closed and I began to sense myself open to the universe without hiding anything within me from it. I couldn't really tell if it was a dream or not, because it was so incredibly lucid. This experience continued until it felt like I was connected to everything that existed through small streams of energy or light. This web of light was a soft, conscious energy; it flowed between me and everything else in existence. It was a most wonderful experience, one that made me aware that, as part of the intelligent universe, it was my duty to make sure that any thoughts or actions I produced were pure and loving. It was like every thought and feeling I had was being shared, and therefore influenced the rest of the universe, and everything else was, in turn, influencing me. The incredible responsibility each of us has as far as the patterns of thoughts and energy we contribute seemed staggering to me. So I kept a tight watch on myself to keep from negatively affecting the universal pool of energy in which we all exist.

I kept my motives pure and tried not to let anything come into my mind that would cause any disturbance, such as anger or emotional fluctuation. This new way of moving through life—forming fewer thoughts and having limited turbulent emotions—was not easy, because it was all so new to me, but I relished the challenge of it. Besides, going back to the old way of doing things was just no longer an option. That "old" personality I had worked so hard to project and maintain in the world no longer existed; a more universal and compassionate Brian was now in his place.

I wasn't really sure what had occurred on that grand night, and I wondered if I had experienced some sort of *kundalini* awakening, like I'd read about. *Kundalini* is described by Eastern mystics as the dominate life-force energy of Self that resides coiled in the lower portions of the spinal column, which when activated, rises up through the seven meridian centers or *chakras* of the body. This activation can occur spontaneously, or through following a spiritual path. Upon activation, which can occur spontaneously or be cultivated through the evolution of the spiritual path, the energy rises up through the seven meridian centers or "chakras," as they are called.

Once this energy is pulsating throughout one's physical being, it produces profound mystical and spiritual effects, but can also create problems within the physical or subtle body. I had read several books on Eastern philosophy and yoga that mentioned the *kundalini* experience, but there were no experts around with whom I could discuss it and receive the proper guidance.

I even had to consider whether or not I had a "walk-in" experience happen to me, and to tell you the truth I wasn't really sure. There were metaphysical stories and books I had read about a phenomenon called "walk-ins." This has to do with the theory that a person can voluntarily choose to have their consciousness and life force/soul, leave their body and allow another consciousness and life force to step in to take it over for the remainder of the body's lifespan. The one who leaves their body has either completed the work they came to do, or the life they signed up for was just too damn hard and they offered to take permanent leave and try again later. I sometimes chuckle when I walk by hair salons and see signs in the window saying that "walk-ins are welcome."

As time passed after my "experience," it seemed to me that most of society was moving in a direction that I did not want to go in, and I felt like an outsider. Humanity, or at least those in positions of influence within humanity, seemed bent on messing up the planet with pollution, greed, and disharmony, and I wanted no part of it. And so I started resisting society in my own way. And I soon made some other major changes in my life so that I would be aligned with my new attitude and state of mind. The first change I made was with my diet—I became a vegetarian. I did that to be peaceful to all living things. The next move was to start wearing only natural fiber clothing, which went against all of my mother's conditioning and expectations. She could not stand wrinkled clothing at all. I guess you could say that sewing was her tennis and polyester was her Ping-Pong!

Because I was now having to deal with final exams and keep myself somewhat together, there was no time to process what had happened to me during my altered state that night in the dorm. I would have preferred to spend time adjusting to what had happened but I needed to hit the road. I had 10 days before I had to leave the States and stay with my father for the summer at his new post. So I caught a Greyhound bus to Iowa and visited my brother. That would give me a little time to decompress. He was raising pit bulls and supervising cable television construction crews with people he hired from the local prisons. He had become a legend in the industry by now and his nickname was "King Cable."

Once I was at Danny's and was sitting on his couch, he handed me a vodka gimlet and a book. "Here's a book from a spiritual group that gave it to me at the airport."

"Thanks, I'll take a look at it. I have never read anything from this guy."

He had no further need for it, and so I spent some time thumbing through it. When it was time to plan dinner, I explained to my brother that I was now a vegetarian. He told me in a half-joking tone, "Hey Swami, whenever you stay with me the rule is you'll have to eat red meat and smoke cigarettes!" We both laughed. At the end of our time together he took me to the bus station and said mockingly, and almost prophetically, "See you later, Swami."

Once I was back at home, a plane ticket arrived for me in the mail. Then my official passport came that provided me with diplomatic immunity stamped with fresh visas. I was ready to head out to spend the summer with Dad in the Middle East at his final post before retirement. He was my financial benefactor and expected me to join him. Soon I was soaring in a plane above the clouds where I could gain some perspective on life down below. I needed to make some sense out of what had happened to me that night at the dorm. I needed to learn how to adjust to this new mode of awareness that came with a sense of being "at One" with everything. As exquisite as it was in terms of being in a state of expanded consciousness, it was also frightening and lonely. I still needed to function in day-to-day life with the rest of the world, which didn't seem to be operating from that same type of conscious knowingness.

With my brother Danny, 1979 (Credit – Norma Johnson)

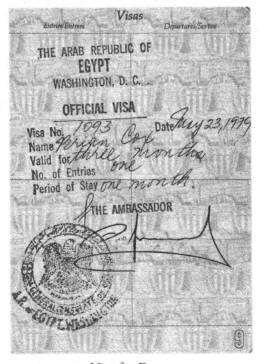

Visa for Egypt

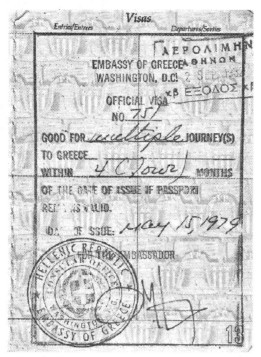

Visas for Greece

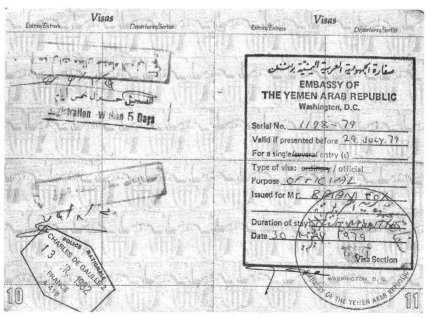

Visa for the Yemen Arab Republic

CHAPTER 6

Tennis in the Land of Sheba

Reclining in my seat on the final leg of the flight to visit with Dad for the summer, I mentally prepared myself for what was to come: the daily challenge of life with his unpredictable moods. He had never used physical abuse against me as far as I can remember, but his emotional states could be quite caustic. As the stewardess gave us landing instructions and the jet descended, I looked out upon the stark, barren landscape and cliffs of North Yemen.

Yemen was spoken of by the ancient Romans as "Arabia Felix," which means "Happy Arabia." The capital city of the Yemen Arab Republic, Sana'a, had been inhabited since before the time of Jesus but a few hundred years of strife and misfortune had taken its toll on the Yemen people, as well as their landscape. First, it was the poorest country in the Middle East and there was a civil war raging against South Yemen. Also, North Yemen had no natural resources to speak of and the underground water aquifers were dropping. And outside the capital, lawless tribes throughout the country kidnapped tourists to use as bargaining chips in their economic and political demands from the government.

Hoping to play some tennis during my stay, I brought a mid-sized, black, aluminum, Prince racket that a friend from college had traded to me at the last minute. The Yonex I was using at the time had popped a string and so I had to let it go. With racket in hand, I exited the plane, walked across the tarmac, and came into the terminal to go through the custom's search.

Inside the terminal, the Yemeni men looked as weathered and rugged as the cliffs I had seen from the air. Many of them wore long skirts and sport coats that could have come from a thrift store. I put my hand on the counter and noticed that it was coated with a layer of very fine, gritty dust. *Must be from the sand that blows down from Saudi Arabia*, I thought. It turns out that everything is Yemen gets coated with this fine layer of grit. There is no escape from it. Dad was outside the customs area, so I headed that way when I saw him wave through the glass partition.

When we got close we shook hands and he looked me over. "Hey, buddy! You look good. How much do you weigh?"

"About 140."

"Oh, too bad," he said. "That's too light for my division. I'm up to about 152 now," he explained with a comical frown, as he patted his stomach to show where the extra weight was. "Are you hungry?" he asked.

"No, I ate on the plane."

"Here, let me have your suitcase. The car is this way. Have you been massaging your scalp? Your hair looks kind of puny."

"I know, I need to floss more, too," I replied.

We went through the exit doors and were met outside by a bright sun. On our way into Sana'a, Yemeni women drifted along the sidewalks covered from head to toe in black fabric. Another new sight was the flurry of plastic shopping bags that blew down every street. Apparently there was a new bag factory on the edge of town and it seemed the bags had now become the unofficial national bird. Red, blue, and yellow ones drifted from place to place as gusts of wind and dust devils sent them fleeing from their perches.

As we drove to his house I asked Dad, "So what is your job like here?"

"Well, we have a program that sends Yemeni college students to America for several years of training. When they return home, they serve their country for two years in their areas of expertise. It's a good cause, but it has its problems."

Dad had never spoken with me about any of his previous jobs or projects, so I figured this was a nice opportunity to keep the conversation going.

"What are the problems?"

"Ah, hell, Brian. You don't really want to know," he replied, as if he was sure I was not sincerely interested. I had spent so many years trying to get away from my father, and now I was trying to get closer to him, but he was resisting. I knew that he was closing himself off from any meaningful discussions.

Changing the subject, he spoke again. "Did you see the knives the Yemeni men wear in their waistbands?" he asked. "Those are *jambiyas*. When they pull a *jambiya* from the sheath they must draw blood."

"Really?" I replied. "Thanks for warning me. This place looks and feels like we stepped back in time a few hundred years. Is there a Ping-Pong table in town?"

"Yeah, buddy. There's a table at the Marine House," he replied in a friendlier tone. "We'll go there this weekend," he confirmed as his face lit up with the prospect of playing as doubles partners again.

"Brian, look at the bundles of green leaves those men are carrying. It's *khat*, a narcotic plant they chew on every day. Every afternoon when the cannon goes off at the *souk* in the old city they all rush out to buy it, and then go back home to chew it and drink tea for hours."

We finally arrived at my father's house, and because I was tired from many hours of traveling, I went to bed soon after. As I lay resting in my dad's spare bedroom, I could hear prayer calls ringing out all over the city through crackly speakers placed high in the minarets of the mosques. As much as I would have preferred to take a break from having to think about higher consciousness and God, I was unable to avoid it.

For the next few days, Dad gave me the rundown on Yemen. He worked at the USAID compound on the road that led toward the airport. The phone system in Yemen was not reliable so, as official personnel, we were given two-way radios to use at home along with a sheet of code names to employ instead of offering up our real ones. Our units were always turned on and anyone who listened overheard everyone else's conversations. Announcements updated us when military actions were taking place outside the city so that trouble spots could be avoided. If you were already out on the road it was best to avoid certain areas if tanks were spotted. You could never count on knowing which side they were on.

There was a single asphalt tennis court inside the U.S. Embassy grounds right beside the ambassador's residence. The residence was a classic Yemeni structure made of hand-cut stones. It stood about five stories high land looked like a giant gingerbread house.

On our first weekend morning at eight o'clock sharp, just after we had breakfast and Dad performed the ritual of massaging his scalp, he and I jumped into his beat up purple Toyota station wagon with faux wood door panels, packed some cold beers into a cooler, and headed over to the court. Tennis was one of the main social functions for expats and visitors. A challenge ladder was posted on a board outside the court with around 17 nametags on it. George Lane, the U.S. Ambassador, held the top spot.

Dad pointed George out to me while he was on the court playing doubles with the first group. Large-framed and tall, he had a distinctive, Ivy League look with dark but graying hair. He appeared to be in his late 50s, which was my Dad's age, and carried himself regally in a relaxed, self-assured manner. Below him on the challenge ladder was a cadre of seasoned players. The British had a court at their Embassy as well and a small group played for their flag at an annual tournament. Dad said that since the American players outnumbered the ones from other countries, "the tournament is a team affair with the Americans against the Brits and everyone else."

To accommodate as many people as possible, the first tennis matches of the morning were doubles. The top group included the ambassador, the administrative officer, and a tall USAID employee who played with an oversized Prince aluminum. I had never seen a racket with a face so huge. With his long wingspan and stride USAID man covered most of the court with about two steps in any direction and was a ferocious poacher at the net. After watching a few games I could see that even with my new racket it was going to take everything I had to contend with the top players. After the primary group had played their matches, others were invited onto the court by the tennis leaders. I studied everyone's games immediately and took mental note of their tendencies and capabilities. The group took pleasure in crafting competitive match-ups. This informal system seemed to work well, and everyone got to play against different combinations of teams.

Dad and I were immediately paired as a doubles team. We proved to be formidable, knowing one another's timing and shots so well. With every really good point I made, I could see Dad's admiration show through his crusty shell and I was pleased. After the matches everyone sat under the shade trees, enjoyed a beer or two, and talked about life in Yemen.

As far as singles matches went, my plan was to hang back and not make a challenge onto the tennis ladder. If I lost on the initial challenge match, I would have to start at the bottom and I was unwilling to suffer that indignity. Challenging the big players directly would have appeared as though I was coming from a sense of needing to beat them, and I wanted none of that. Plus I needed time to maximize what I could do with the new racket. So I decided to draw the top players out slowly and pick them off one at a time like Clint Eastwood in a Sergio Leone western.

The U.S. Marines who guarded the Embassy lived in a two-story house inside a small compound on the outside of Ring Road, which surrounded the city. Marine House parties were typically held every weekend at every American Embassy post around the world. So Dad and I headed there to party and play some Ping-Pong after we had dinner and did the dishes. (My father was too disciplined to ever let the dishes sit in the sink.)

David Farrington, one of the marines I had met earlier, greeted me when Dad and I arrived at the party. "Hey, Brian. Glad you came early. Oh, no! You have your own paddle in a special case, too?" He asked in amazement.

"Of course. I need every advantage I can get!" It was actually one of my father's back-up paddles.

Dave turned to my father and said jokingly, "Hey Dan, do you carry a gun in your case? Jostling with him in a friendly manner he continued, "Because I think you should."

"Hey, Mark! How are you, my good friend? No, there's no gun. When I learned how to kill a man with my bare hands I quit carrying one," Dad replied with a chuckle, but confident that he could back up those words if he had to. He knew that his knockout punch was still capable of producing serious damage or even death.

Laughing, Mark retorted, "You are too funny! What can I get you to drink?"

"Why thank you. I'll have a whiskey and a splash of branch water on ice, if you could be so kind."

My father was congenial with people whom he thought took a liking to him, yet hypersensitive to, and on the lookout for, even the smallest of perceived slights or one-upmanship that came his way.

That evening Dad and I took on all challengers into the wee hours of the morning—and we never lost a match at the Marine House for the rest of the summer. It felt great playing doubles with him again and to see him smile when we won points and games against some of the best players. Since Yemen was in such a remote location, there was always an unusual mix of people at the Marine House parties and other functions. There were U.S. fighter jet pilots who were training the Yemeni squadrons, USAID staff, Peace Corps volunteers, NGO charity employees, and on rare occasion a few visiting stewardesses who enjoyed rock star attention.

Even though it was an Islamic country and the Yemenis were not allowed to have any, discreet shipments of alcohol were brought in each year for families on official assignment. After the plane landed, cases of precious liquid cargo were transferred into a large truck and covered with tarps to prevent the public from being offended. Armed guards rode on the truck to the USAID compound and orders were filled. The cabinets at his house looked like a duty-free liquor store filled with cases of Budweiser, Heineken, vodka, gin, whiskey, wine, and the like.

After a few weeks, some of the tennis regulars became a little restless and eager to test their games against me in singles. The best players at the top of the ladder held back, but a few were willing to make their move; when the competitive tension finally pushed them over the edge, they stepped forward and confronted me for a game. The first regular who wanted a serious match with me was Mona. She was the cheerful wife of one of the communication officers, and was probably in her late 30s. Mona spent a lot of time and effort working on her game and was a good athlete; I could see her improving each week. She had solid strokes, foot speed, and was extremely consistent. Without a lot of oomph behind her shots, her strategy was to hit from the baseline, and stay in each point without going for any winners until the opponent made a mistake. She was just the kind of steady player who could wreak havoc on my game.

One Saturday, Mona approached me under the trees by the court. "So, Brian, are we going to play a set sometime?"

"Are you sure you're ready for this? I don't back down from official challenges."

"Then I'm officially challenging," she said.

So we settled on a time and date for the match. People in the tennis community were excited because it was going to be one of those Bobby Riggs/Billy Jean King spectacles. I'm sure they wanted to see Rosalie take me down. She was the underdog, and I was the cocky college kid with a flashy game and no job.

I had been working on a John McEnroe service motion by using a couple forward dips before the toss. Part of my game plan was to get Mona used to the timing of two dips, and then I would throw some ones and threes at her as a surprise to throw her off.

The match began with cautious tennis; I knew Mona always played conservatively, so I didn't want to make too many unforced errors and fall right into her trap. We both made our shots like chess moves, thinking each one out with deliberate execution. I took a little speed off my first serves to keep the percentage high and used the McEnroe service dips, varying the number of them to throw off her timing.

The points became the mini-marathons I'd expected, but I was able to gain momentum as the match wore on. In the end, Mona became exhausted from the long rallies and couldn't maintain her level of play.

A small crowd cheered for her but it was not enough to prevent the inevitable. I wasn't pleased to beat her—it would have meant a lot to her to win, but holding back to be gentlemanly and losing this one wasn't acceptable to me, either. But she accepted the loss gracefully and we became hitting partners for the rest of the summer.

When the time came for the summer tournament against the international community, the tennis ladder rankings were used for picking the U.S. team. The American ambassador was the top singles player, and the rest of the crew filled in behind. Although I had not challenged onto the ladder, I was picked to play mixed-doubles with the ambassador's wife. Having never practiced or played together, we were an interesting but ultimately losing combination. The American team came out on top at the end of the matches, and the hosts at the British Embassy threw a small party afterward with drinks, food, and dart games, which they easily won as a tradition.

Without a job I had time to explore the country when the opportunity arose. At one party I had the good fortune to meet a young Egyptian man about my age named Marwan. A few days each week he borrowed his uncle's Mercedes sedan with diplomatic plates and we flew down the dirt roads at reckless speeds, past ancient villages, spinning the car in circles until dust poured into the open windows until we were laughing and coughing hard at the same time.

During a party at the Marine House one evening my friend Marwan walked in looking like he could use a strong drink.

"Hey, Brian!"

"Marwan, good to see you."

"We looked for you last weekend between Mokha and Kokha."

"Really? We camped on the beach north of the army installation we came across in the middle of the night. We were almost mistaken for intruders and shot."

"Yes, Carlos and Kathleen packed up a Suburban after we heard you were going out there. We couldn't find you and the second day our vehicle was stuck up to the axles in quicksand."

"It took us hours to get across the Tehama with all those damn palm tree holes. How did you get out?"

"We saw a small speck in the distance and it was a villager. After about three or four hours of hiking he came over to us. He offered to get us out for 25,000 rials. I bargained him down to 17,000 and he went back and got a bunch of people from the village. They lifted us out and put palm tree branches down in front of the Suburban so we could keep moving."

We toasted drinks to our good fortune.

"Brian," he told me, "you'll have to come to Cairo some time and stay at our place. I'll show you the city and you are always welcome."

"Thanks, Marwan. That would be great. I'll see what I can do."

One of the highlights for me that summer was a road trip to the city of Shibam and the mountaintop village of Kawkaban. Carlos was an NGO employee who had been in the country a few years and Kathleen, a young American about 19 years old who was visiting her mother, took a day trip with me there. We headed out of town in my old man's purple, Toyota station wagon with the faux wood-grain panels. Along the way I put on some tapes of The Alan Parsons Project and The Cars' debut album, which made traveling through the lunar-like landscape even more surreal.

We cruised through barren valleys with green patches of *khat* gardens here and there and wound our way along the black ribbon of asphalt until we finally reached the village of Shibam, with its high-rise buildings that are made of dirt.

The small shops we pulled up to were located near the base of steep rock cliffs. At the top sat the village of Kawkaban. Carlos said we should hike up the steep, rocky trail, which had quite a few sharp switchbacks and no handrails. Kathleen was a pack a day cigarette smoker and resistant to the whole idea. But after much prodding, she agreed to give it a go. We took a couple of breaks along the way, and after we passed through the stone arch at the very top, with Kathleen trailing behind us and gasping for oxygen, we were rewarded for our effort with an incredible view. We walked near a water cistern, and several barefoot children rushed over to greet us.

Doug greeted them in Arabic, "*Salaam ahlay-koom.*"

"*Wah-ahlay koom-salaam,*" they responded and giggled.

The people in this area had retreated to these massive cliffs to escape the brutalities inflicted by various attackers over the centuries. We snapped pictures of the kids with our instant Polaroid that produced hard copy photos with the touch of a buttom.

"Shukraan! Shukraan!" they exclaimed with glee and amazement at seeing what they looked like in the photographs.

"Marhabaan bik," Carlos replied.

These were the types of kids Dad had served most of his professional life: the ones who knew, like he had during his youth, that life is truly hard. For many it only comes with brief moments of relief. We enjoyed a walking tour of the village with Carlos and headed down the mountain trail before darkness fell. But we were careful, as one misstep on the trail could lead to serious injury, and decent medical care would have been hours away.

By the time summer ended I had fallen in love with the Yemeni people and this hard-luck country that seemed lost in time. But it was time for me to go back to school. When I said my goodbyes, the Marine gunnery sergeant at the Embassy stopped to speak with me by the main gate.

"Brian, when you get back to the States, look for a book called *Shibumi*," he said. "I really think you'll like it."

From our conversations at the Marine House parties, the gunnery sergeant knew I was interested in the field of human potential as well as philosophical subjects. "I will, Gunny. Hold down the fort until I make it back." Before I turned away, I straightened up and saluted him.

My time in Yemen had been successful in multiple ways. I felt more comfortable with my new state of awareness, and I had also kept my inner reactions calm in the face of Dad's often childlike mood swings. A huge bonus was that from gradually becoming stronger as partner's on the court and on the Ping-Pong table, I could see Dad and I were more accepting of each other…enough to give me hope that we could build on that newfound respect, if only he would allow it.

A view of Sana'a, Yemen

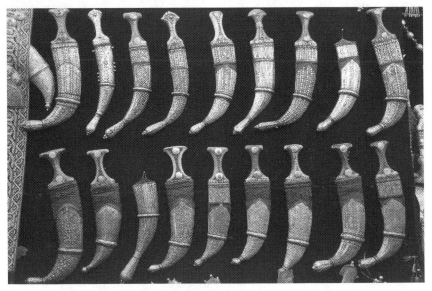

Traditional Yemeni jambiya daggers with handles that
are unfortunately made of rhinoceros horn

The mountaintop village of Kawkaban, Yemen

Visa for the Yemen Arab Republic

CHAPTER 7

The Death of Tennis in North Yemen

Back in the Pacific Northwest I moved into the dorm I had lived in before and took several religious courses. Yes, *The Bible* had some incredible stories and lessons in it, but my heart and mind had always been more inclined toward Eastern perspectives. But unfortunately, a full load of academic courses and my participation in the intramural sports program left me little time to further investigate what specific practices and wisdom of the East had to offer me in terms of understanding and adjusting to my new state of sensitive awareness and expanded awareness. I wanted to keep some of that awareness open, but not enough to make my daily life impossible. It felt like I was straddling two worlds at the same time, riding on the razor's edge.

Each fall, intramural flag football games were played at night on a field made from crushed bricks that shredded skin on contact. Looked like fun to me! My friend, Steve Thomas, and I had formed a team made up of fellow underclassmen, eager to prove themselves against the established teams. The most fearsome teams were juggernauts with NFL-sized rosters and ringers. And when the behemoths from those teams led a sweep to your side like rampaging warriors, you had better have signed up for additional student health insurance!

Fortunately, I was on my father's insurance plan. After a nasty head-to-head collision during a game one night, I was laid out cold and was having multiple seizures. The ambulance arrived and emergency responders took me to three hospitals before they found one with the expertise and the equipment needed for my condition. My teammates and friends in the dorm prayed for me, and I stayed in a comatose state for what may have been a day or two. Mom came up from Oregon to be with me in the hospital and to consult with the doctors.

All I remember about the incident was a day or so later when I began regaining consciousness and was becoming aware that I was rejoining my body. My immediate feeling was that I was returning to my body from a place of total unconditional love. I was conscious of my existence but I was not in my body just yet. As I came back in I promised that I would hold onto and remember that experience of feeling total love and continue to embody it as much as possible for the rest of my existence on Earth. Before I even tried to move a muscle or open my eyes, my lips smiled as I let myself open to the new possibilities I was going to have now. With a new lease on life, I had nothing to lose. I knew that it was now time to live on my terms as much as possible, no matter what anybody else thought.

The doctors gave me some anti-seizure medicine and told me not to risk another head injury any time soon. I disregarded their advice and scored a touchdown against one of the top teams on a trick play where we had somebody run out of bounds after the huddle and I stealthily emerged onto the field from the opposite sideline and caught the pass. We didn't win the game but we proved that the best teams would have to contend with us nipping at their heels. A few of our friends then formed teams for the basketball, volleyball, softball, and other sports tournaments the next two quarters and competed each week, becoming more familiar with each other's capabilities and winning a fair share of the games.

The next summer came around and a plane ticket and my passport arrived in the mail with fresh visas once again. It was time to return to North Yemen but the situation in that part of the world wasn't good. The American Embassy in Pakistan had just been attacked. The U.S. Ambassador to Afghanistan had been killed in a raid by Afghani troops sent to free him from kidnappers. The Shah of Iran and his group, who were supported by the United States, had been overthrown and the American Embassy personnel in Tehran were being held as hostages. It was not exactly the golden age in the Middle East for American Foreign

Service brats, but I had no alternative; Dad expected me to go and I was up for the adventure.

The mighty Prince racket I had used the previous summer broke a string before my trip, and I traded it for a Jack Kramer just before departing. It was a downgrade going back to a wooden racket with a smaller frame, but I knew there would be no extra rackets in Sana'a. The Kramer was a racket from glory days gone by but it was still capable in the right hands.

Before my flight, I located a copy of *Shibumi*, the book the gunny sergeant in Sana'a had recommended to me—it was the best novel I had ever read. The main character, Nicolai, was an assassin who became a student of the Japanese board game Go, and was skilled at killing people whom he believed, through their despicable actions, deserved that form of karmic return. He saw life through the strategic eyes of a Go master and was proficient in the art of the "naked kill," the ability to create a deadly weapon from any available item within reach.

With his highly developed extrasensory skills, Nicolai was also one of the world's most artful lovers. As he grew older, though, he lost contact with an inner state of transcendence that he could previously access. The artful lover part with his lady friend sounded intriguing; but unfortunately, Nicolai didn't share the most intimate secrets of his lovemaking or killing techniques; both were far too dangerous for the clumsy and untrained.

I ran into the gunny sergeant my first week back in Yemen and thanked him for referring the book. When I was recruited as a ringer for grudge tennis matches in Yemen, it seemed that in a way I was like Nicolai: an assassin brought in to deliver a karmic blow…I was just doing it through tennis. And similarly, Nicolai and I both longed for a transcendent state of wholeness we once had access to in our youth.

There was significant news to report since my last visit to Sana'a: Dad had remarried. After seeing a few of their pictures around the house, I could see that he and his new wife had known each other since the 1960s. No wonder he had been so difficult with us all those years! Now it all made sense. He had been frustrated living a double life. I guess Mom, Jean, Danny, and I were just Dad's non-essential personnel.

Nevertheless, I tried not to let any awkwardness get in the way, and the three of us began life together under one roof.

Their new house was just a few blocks off of Wadi Dahr Road next to what looked like one of the oldest cemeteries in the city. A small butcher shop sat on the corner at Wadi Dahr Road. Raw meat hung on hooks outside, coated with equal amounts of dust and flies, and nobody seemed to mind the stray dogs who picked through the garbage for their next meal.

The yard around the house was surrounded by high security walls and lights every five feet. A large pomegranate bush was bursting with softball-sized fruit near the front metal gate. The house had been nicely outfitted by the previous USAID facilities director who had moved on to Sudan. Dad's new house also featured a large screened-in patio with beautiful grape vines cascading from the roof, ripe with purple bunches of grapes. A bristle dartboard was set up on the patio as it had been on all of our posts in the past, and Dad played the same honky-tonk albums I had heard for years. They had grown on me by now, and I knew them all by heart.

But best of all by far was the living room with a high ceiling where Dad had set up a Ping-Pong table. There were only two tables that I knew of in Sana'a and we had one of them. Now that was some awesome table tennis karma! As soon as I arrived, our training sessions and friendly rivalry was renewed. Some nights we would hit for hours doing the drills we'd always done. Getting faster and faster we'd gather enough control to keep the rally going until someone missed. There was little talking. When we did play a game, every point was hard fought yet there was plenty of light-hearted laughter after good points. Dad could no longer keep up with my level of speed and creative shot-making but he didn't seem to mind anymore when I beat him. We remained silent about it, but it seemed like there was an understanding that our sessions were making both of our games stronger. So we continued pushing each other to faster slams, more effective chops, and serves with as much spin as we could impart. Dad was actually getting so good that it took everything I had to beat him! After playing he would fix his nightly drinks, listen to his honky-tonk music, and we would play darts the way we had a thousand times before.

Not long after my arrival, Dad threw a small party and introduced me to some of the other expats with the hope that I would find a job and not just lounge around the tennis court like last year. I learned there was a position open at the U.S. Embassy and, after an interview with the Administrative Officer and staff, I accepted the offer to join them. The Embassy complex appeared very vulnerable, and one afternoon we practiced our escape and evacuation plan. If the camel dung really hit the fan, I knew the scene wouldn't go down like the practice walk-through at all. The Embassy was one of the most exposed compounds in the world, and everyone knew it. We were Benghazi waiting to happen.

There were several operational functions I handled at the Embassy. One of the duties was riding a Yamaha 200 motorbike each day to the various travel agencies and government offices to deliver and pick up documents. The Yemenis loved racing against me on the streets, and they smiled and laughed at the intersections when I revved the engine to signal I was up for another scramble. Drivers and motorbike riders were usually close to crashing into one another while simultaneously honking, yelling, and chewing *khat* with little regard for rules. It was a spectacle!

Dad and I played less tennis together as he now spent more of his time teaching his new wife how to play. I joined them when I could, and we worked with her until she had the basics down. I was also coming to terms with the fact that all those years of them keeping their relationship a secret had been hard on all of us; yet all of a sudden she was now my new stepmother and tennis buddy. She was a gracious person and doted on Dad, so I figured that as long as they were happy and Mom back in Oregon had gained her own freedom, everything may have just worked out perfectly for everyone.

By the end of the summer, it was clear that Dad and I were one of the strongest doubles teams, only losing a rare set here or there. Dad was never one to hand out compliments, but he gave me a few "nice shots" during points when I made a particularly good one, and I returned the compliments to him as well when he deserved them.

Near the end of summer Ambassador Lane approached me at the court one morning. I guess the growing competitive tension had pushed him over the edge. Number One finally had to know if he could beat me or not. And so he asked, "Brian, would you be available to play some singles with me on Wednesday afternoon? At three o'clock?"

"Yes, I would, Mr. Ambassador," I said, accepting the challenge.

"Fine, we'll see you then." He then walked toward the Chancery. The showdown was finally going to happen. I felt as ready as I could be and Dad was the most excited I had ever seen him about one of my matches. He gave me instructions to call him on the two-way radio after the match and communicate a secret coded message to him if I won.

The night before our match, Ambassador Lane and his family had us over for dinner, after which we watched the movie *Klute*. What are the odds of being in a remote place like Yemen and hearing a line in a movie about being in a remote place like Yemen? Everyone laughed when we heard it.

Our big match was scheduled at a time when the weekend crowd would not be around to watch and I was happy about that. That took some of the pressure off me because I knew most of the people would be cheering and pulling for the ambassador and I didn't want to be affected by any of that. At the appointed time the next day, the match got underway. The look on George's face told me he was very serious about this match. He was very focused. This match would decide who the unofficial champion of Yemen truly was.

We both placed our shots most carefully at the beginning and didn't go for too much. I wasn't ready to create unforced errors and squander any points. Taking down Ambassador Lane would be a crown jewel in my non-illustrious tennis career, maybe even bigger than beating Dad. George put everything he had into moving his large frame around the asphalt faster than I expected and returned my shots with his herky-jerky movements.

I popped in my first serves with good pace, and he blocked them back with more ease than I expected. As each point developed, I ran him right and left to the corners. I threw in some drop shots, lobs, and passing shots to mix things up. George was soon sweating and was working much harder than I think he was used to, but he wasn't going to crack easily. So I hugged the baseline and started taking the balls early, and put more emphasis on dictating the rallies instead of being overly cautious. Though most of the points were close, I had the advantage on the big ones and finally broke his serve. First set to Mr. Cox, thank you very much.

I did my best to look as calm as I could but the weight of the moment was growing and I felt the pressure increase. I have noticed after years of playing in tough situations that, the more the psychological pressure builds, the more every small defect in your game becomes magnified. My backhand was my biggest weakness and so I covered it up at all cost, slicing when he hit it to that side, and ran around to hit forehands whenever I could. I was becoming more aggressive with each point, whipping in some heavy topspin forehands that came from my table tennis training. Rafael Nadal would have enjoyed seeing those shots.

As the sweat continued to pour from both of our brows, a breeze ruffled through the leaves on the shade trees, and the prayer calls crackled out over the city. As I was getting ready to serve out the match the political officer walked over from the Chancery and approached the court. He spoke through the fence quietly to the Ambassador. Ambassador Lane then walked up to the net and said to me, "I'm very sorry, Brian, but I'm going to have to leave. There is something I must attend to."

"I understand, sir. We'll have to play again sometime," I offered.

"Let's do that." He shook my hand and then walked off the court and got into his chauffeured car with his bodyguard. We never got the opportunity to finish the match and neither of us reached out to play again as if we both knew the outcome would be in my favor once again. I picked up the radio at the Embassy and called in a message to Dad. "Charlie Three to Charlie One. I won't need a ride home. Charlie Three out."

"Charlie One to Charlie Three," he replied. "Copy that. Charlie One out."

That was the signal that I had taken the match and would be walking home. Even though the set had not been completed, I considered it to be a TKO win. I allowed myself a few moments of exaltation in the accomplishment and then left it at that. I knew that it was better to follow the advice of Rudyard Kipling in his epic poem *If*, and not become attached to either winning or losing. Rudyard's famous words greet Wimbledon competitors above the door that leads them out to Center Court. As long as I made the best effort I could, I was satisfied.

The day I was to leave Sana'a, Dad and I shook hands at the airport as he saw me off. He gave me a Dutch-rub on the top of my head with his knuckles and reminded me once again, "Brian, make sure you massage your scalp every week. You need to get your hair more healthy." I nodded in agreement.

As the plane lifted off the ground, I was glad that my father and I were getting along better than ever and, equally so, that he and I would now be on opposite sides of the planet for another nine months.

On the way back to America I routed my flight through Germany to see a girlfriend I had known in Bogota. She tapped me on the shoulder from behind as I was leaving the luggage area. When I turned around, our eyes met. We embraced, kissed and then we were off for a blissful week at her home in Landsberg while her mother was away. The desire to experience intimacy had overcome my sense of wanting to be non-attached to the physical realm quite a bit more easily than I had imagined. I left Germany trying to ignore the obvious fact that teenage love on the run rarely lasted when separated by thousands of miles and different languages and cultures. And in time, much to the dismay of my heart, ours didn't.

***

The university I attended was going to build a larger, more comprehensive intramural sports competition for the students. Tournaments were scheduled and the winning organization each year would have their team name engraved on the President's Trophy. With some excellent recruiting by my friends and some late-night strategizing, we felt ready. Mind you, our organization was a volatile mix of highly charged egos and testosterone. Fights among ourselves were becoming more common, and it was soon my role to be the moderator and peacemaker. Each academic quarter we sacrificed our bodies, and way too much time and money but and at the end of the year our efforts paid off. Our team name was engraved on the President's Trophy and it was displayed in a showcase next to the school's NCAA memorabilia.

And fortunately, I found that as I kept myself busy organizing teams and playing sports instead of seeking higher realms of consciousness, the unusual awakening I had gone through in the dorm several years ago, and its effects, had begun to recede more safely into the background.

***

Summer soon arrived once again, and it was time to fly to North Yemen for the third and last time. The U.S. government has an age limit for Foreign Service dependents and my expiration date was approaching. After moving back into Dad's house I learned that a new ambassador had replaced Ambassador Lane. Spending the first few weekends on the court and watching him play, I could see that the new ambassador didn't have a strong passion for the game. His young daughter and son were just learning and I spent some time on the court with them. I always hit with anyone who asked, no matter their level of play. That was the way I gave back to the sport and helped inspire others to experience the joy of playing it better than they ever thought possible.

The loss of Ambassador Lane as a major tennis force had taken away the outstanding play and matches we had previously known. Most of the old crowd had moved on to new posts, never to be heard from again. Nobody even bothered to take their names off the tennis ladder or schedule challenge matches.

The Embassy hired me into my former position and I was happy to work once again with two Yemeni employees who knew me from before. They risked their lives and families each day to come to work with us and brought in fresh and delicious flatbread for us to eat each morning to enjoy along with the sugary hot tea that is served in Yemen.

The next month a few of us were sitting under the trees next to the tennis court getting ready to play. One of the communications officers walked over from the Chancery and announced to us, "The

Fourth of July celebration has been cancelled. There are reports that a rocket-propelled grenade attack is being planned against the Embassy. Everyone should alter arrival times and paths to work in order to avoid forming a pattern. Be sure to keep your radios on at home."

The RPG attack never happened but a few weeks later a coup d'état was launched against President Saleh and his government. Bursts of gunfire and explosions woke me up, but the commotion ended before sunrise, and that was the last we heard of it. For me, though, the worst news wasn't the party and tennis tournament being cancelled, or even the risk of possible death from an RPG round; I could accept those minor inconveniences and move on. The attack against the U.S. Embassy never happened but a real tragedy occurred when a sinkhole opened up in one of the ad corners of the tennis court. It soon expanded to six feet wide and was becoming harder to avoid.

After someone almost fell in and we lost a few balls to it, we grudgingly surrendered the court to the growing sinkhole; it just became too dangerous to play. To me, at that point, tennis in Yemen had died. Yeah, the new five-star hotel overlooking the city had some brand-new courts and overpriced beer…but those courts had no sanctity. They felt sterile like they had no soul. And so I refused to play there.

The day before I was to leave the country, I rode the Embassy motorbike up the hill beside the new hotel that overlooked the city. Some of us had been in there the night before, listening to a Filipino disco band belt out Donna Summer tunes, while drinking expensive French champagne on the tab of one of our helicopter-pilot contacts who liked to live large. It was sad for me to see Yemen becoming so mainstream.

While sitting on the Yamaha motorbike, I was looking over the city and took in the moment. I acknowledged my appreciation to the universe for everything I had experienced up to this point in time, even the hard times with Dad. Then I drove down the hill and took a final lap around Ring Road. I gunned past the other motorbikes, taxis, and donkey carts from one light to the next, and jockeyed for position in the roundabouts like the chariot race from *Ben-Hur*. In victory I pulled into the parking lot of the Embassy and spun a few doughnuts in front of the Yemeni guards who had known me over the past few years. They raised their rifles and cheered as they always did.

The next morning, Dad drove me out to the airport and shook my hand goodbye. He never gave hugs and wasn't going to start now. Dad looked at me and said with emphasis, "Be a good boy, Brian."

"Yes, sir," I dutifully replied, to show him I remembered his training and would obey his command. If I screwed up it was all on me now. I took my seat on the plane, the engines roared, and we sped down the runway. The nose lifted off and as I looked out the window, the morning sun lit the nearby cliffs with a soft orange glow. The plane stopped in Cairo and I linked up there with a good friend and college teammate who had flown over for a vacation. My Egyptian friend I had met in Yemen, Marwan, gave us a tour of the city and the museum. Then we rode camels for a bit and we went into the Great Pyramid and Menkaure's pyramid at Giza, a lifelong dream of mine. The cool passageways in the pyramids gave us some relief from the scorching sun. I would have loved to spend more time inside them but other groups were waiting to enter. The Sphynx was enthralling and I wandered among the ruins, inhaling the history and majesty of the area with every breath.

After touring the more ancient pyramids at Saqqara, I played a few sets of doubles with the weekend regulars on the clay court at the U.S. Embassy in Cairo. I could tell they were not prepared for extreme tennis and after two sets everyone packed their bags and left.

My friend ended up staying at the Embassy guesthouse while he experienced stomach cramps, fever, and diarrhea from an infection brought on by the impure water.

"Cox," he groaned as he rolled on his bed, doubled over in pain, "How come you aren't sick like me?"

"The bugs in Yemen are stronger than the ones in Egypt," I said with a laugh. It was true.

As September approached, we I headed back home after a brief stay in Europe. We were ready to look up some of the young ladies we were fond of, and make another run at the President's Trophy. Winning the overall sports competition three years in a row would mean the university would have to give us permanent possession of the trophy.

Landscape in Yemen

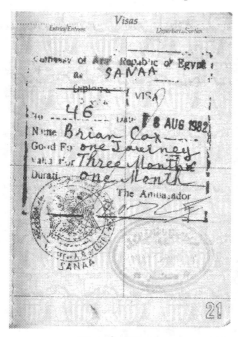

Visa for the Yemen Arab Republic

Visa for Egypt

Yemeni landscape

Riding camels with at the pyramids in Giza with college
friend Tony, 1982 (Credit – Norma Johnson)

At Menkaure's pyramid with our guide

At Menkaure's pyramid with friend Tony and an
unidentified gentleman (Credit – Norma Johnson)

Inside the oldest pyramid at Saqqara, Egypt

CHAPTER 8

Melting Clouds and Choosing a Path

Soon after our return to school, we found that other teams at the university had combined forces to beat us, so our crew scouted as heavily as we could for new talent. One of our recruits had once been on the Miami Dolphins NFL team but he wasn't as fast and aggressive as we had hoped so he didn't get any playing time. Our quarterback for several undefeated years was a former Washington-state basketball champion and NCAA Division I athlete. He stood 6'7" and could throw the football 70 yards, which was the length of the intramural football field. With his psychedelic play calling and a ferocious defense our squad went undefeated and racked up impressive stats in the 7-on-7 games.

Our co-ed volleyball unit squared off against a team that included several members of the Norwegian national team. We won that year's volleyball championship for the first time and finished strong in the other sports. At the end of the year, a group of us gathered to celebrate winning the President's Trophy for the third year in a row. The silver trophy cup was now ours to keep. After college, our team continued to field a football team to defend our streak of football championships but we let go of the other sports. I had been at the center of the whirlwind our team created for so long that after college ended, and all of the excitement dropped away, I didn't know what to do with myself.

I had never prepared myself for a specific career and not having any specific direction after graduation, but being more interested in sports, health and wellness than anything else, I landed a job with a health club, a chain that had indoor tennis courts at multiple locations. One day at work I was given a ticket to a seniors' tennis exhibition tour that was coming to the club. Australian legends like Ken Rosewall, Fred Stolle, John Newcombe, and Rod Laver were set to appear. A few other former top pros were coming, including Stan Smith and Torben Ulrich. I could hardly believe my good fortune.

I told one of my teammates, Scott, about the exhibition and that I was going to watch some the legendary players. He had once beat me 6-0 in a challenge match without even breaking a sweat. Scott had warned me that I wouldn't get a game off him and he was right. That's the thing about tennis: there's always someone better, and if not in this week, then in the next. All tennis fortunes rise and fall like the incoming and outgoing tides. They are bound to nature and entropy, inevitably shifting with the passage of time no matter how brilliant and magnificent they are, or how hard we try to hold onto them. When I told him about the upcoming exhibition he asked me to tell Rod Laver that Scott said "Hello." Scott had once played in the junior leagues in California and apparently had known Rod.

I went to my seat the night of the matches and watched the older pros warm up. They looked surprisingly fit and warmed up in excellent form. The format of the matches was round robin both in the singles and doubles. The tennis was superb and the senior players clearly enjoyed each other's company as they exchanged friendly banter and laughter on the court between points. Their games were much more impressive than I expected. Rosewall won the singles with his strong determination and steady play.

After the event, I walked to my car enjoying the pleasant memories. How often is it that some of the greatest legends in your favorite sport show up where you work and you get to watch them for free? I noticed that another person was heading toward me as I went to my car. As his face became clearer under the lights, I saw that it was Rod Laver. He was walking to his car near where mine was parked. I got closer to him without changing speed or direction as we continued to walk toward each other. I remembered my promise to my friend and said "Mr. Laver, a friend of yours named Scott from Southern California wanted me to say 'Hello' to you for him. And I really enjoyed watching you play tonight."

He looked at me and said, "Thank you very much," and smiled as our eyes met. I didn't hold him up any longer, allowing him to depart without any further delay. I sensed that his rare moments alone were important to him, and so I left it at that and respected his privacy. Just a greeting from an old friend.

I would have loved to play out there with the Australian greats that night and felt I could have held my own against them. Perhaps I'll have to head down to John Newcombe's tennis camp one day if I ever have the opportunity. Beer is part of their post-training regimen and socialization; they sound like my kind of tennis tribe!

At this point in my life, though, what I didn't have was a spiritual teacher or group I could personally relate to and forge ahead with—and I was feeling the need to pick up the search. The Theosophical Society bookstore on Capitol Hill in Seattle was nearby and turned out to be a good resource, so I visited often. I attended a few of their lectures and was intrigued by their history. The society had been formed by the Russian mystic Madame Blavatsky and several others in British colonial India in the late 1800s. She and her partners were allegedly in contact with several mahatmas, great souls, who were trained in occult knowledge and passed their knowledge on for the benefit of humanity.

I read parts of *The Secret Doctrine* and some of her other works, but she often used Sanskrit terminology and concepts with which I was unfamiliar. There were accusations of charlatanism regarding her work, but she and the group had continued on anyway, passing the torch to Annie Besant and others who followed. The Dalai Lama mentioned in one of his books that a visit to the Theosophical Society in India in 1956 showed him that various spiritual traditions contain immense value and that Buddhism was not the only true religion.

Seeking more knowledge, I immersed myself in Thomas Cleary's translations of the Eastern classics such as *Transmission of Light*. It contained stories of the initial awakening of enlightenment from the Buddha down through 53 successive generations of the lineage's top meditation masters, the special ones who became holders of the tradition. The wisdom and dialogues contained in the book were phenomenal.

I immensely enjoyed reading about the grand lineage from India of Babaji, Lahiri Mahasaya, Yukteswar, and Yogananda. When Yogananda brought his teachings to America in the 1930s, he toured the grounds of the Mount Washington Hotel in Los Angeles. As the story goes, he touched the fence of the tennis court and said to his group that this place felt like "the one." Soon after his announcement, the resort became the headquarters for the American branch of his organization, the Self-Realization Fellowship. I would have loved to have played some tennis and studied with Yogananda.

During this period, I also read a few books from a spiritual group which was led by Elizabeth Claire Prophet. Elizabeth had taken over the leadership duties from her husband Mark after he made his final transition. She claimed to trance channel many other beings, including many I had not heard of. Her books were intriguing, so I went to several of their public presentations to find out more. Curious to find out more about the group, I flew to Los Angeles to attend their annual summer conference held on their property north of the city.

Coming onto the grounds the first day of the conference, I saw hundreds of people swarming around in a circus-like atmosphere. Many people sat on folding chairs under big tents, and Elizabeth was shown to us via a television set on a small stage. Initially, like their books, the material seemed profound; but after a while, it became as monotonous as Elizabeth's monotonic, droning voice. But I continued to wander the grounds, and drank some wheatgrass juice at one of the booths. A few of their followers from Seattle spotted me, and we headed out for lunch in one of their cars. They surprised me by launching into high-speed spiritual decrees as soon as the car went into gear. Evidently, they couldn't even get out of the parking lot without Lord Michael affirmations to keep us free from a fender bender. It was at this point that I could see they were a group I would not be interested in spending much time with.

The rest of my family had their own lives changing and evolving while I was searching for a spiritual direction to follow. Mom was working as a secretary in Oregon and was slowly rebuilding her life. A USAID friend of our family from the Taiwan days in the 1960s, Robert Johnson, was in touch with her. During his long career in the Foreign Service, Bob and his family had been on tours of duty in countries such as Greece, Iran, Pakistan, and India. After Bob's wife passed away, he and Mom continued their friendship. They went on a group trip to Greece together and began spending more time together within their social circle. In 1985, Bob accepted a position as a consultant working with the Egyptian government. He invited Mom to join him in Cairo, she accepted and they were married there.

I was thrilled for Mom, and glad to see that she was with such a fine man. After all the years of suffering under my father's "Jekyll and Hyde" behavior, Mom was now exploring archeological digs with Bob, and enjoying the envious swirl of life well lived in Egypt. My brother was still raising pit bull dogs and stringing up cable television systems across America with people he hired out of jails. It was a rough and nasty job but his legendary pole climbing skills led many in the industry to give him the nickname, "King Cable." My sister was a single mom, raising her two boys.

I, of course, was still checking out the philosophy and health selections in some of the local bookstores, I found some books published by an educational group that focused on Eastern philosophy and yoga. They also offered a range of educational and integrated therapeutic programs at their headquarters. The founder was a guru from the Himalayas. He had spent time with various meditation masters in the various regions of India. One of his books described living in the caves and mountains and meeting with fascinating characters like the Devraha Baba—who was said to be over 150 years old—and the adept known as Hariakhan Baba. He had also spent time with Gandhi, Aurobindo, Swami Brahmananda, and Anandamayi Ma, who came to be known as the "Hugging Saint."

The organization also offered an experiential graduate program in Eastern studies in cooperation with an accredited university. I began to seriously consider whether something like that would be possible for me.

Sitting outside one afternoon, I looked up at some small, puffy clouds and remembered a technique from one of the books I had read on human potential. It mentioned using the power of the mind to melt clouds and I decided to try it. Focusing my eyes on one small, fluffy cloud, I paid attention to it as if I were beaming energy toward it. Over the course of several minutes, I watched the cloud slowly disappear while other clouds right beside it were still there. I tried the technique again on another cloud and got the same positive result.

After one more afternoon of melting clouds, just to make sure it wasn't my imagination, it was clear to me that the focused mind could affect things outside of the body. If the power of the mind could alter clouds, I knew it could be used for all kinds of things and that I needed to seriously apply myself to learning what was truly possible. So I placed an order for one of the guru's guided meditation tapes for beginners. I was taking my first baby steps toward becoming a yogi but I had to start somewhere. I had to look the part, too, so I also bought a handmade backpack from Tibet and a T-shirt with some spiritual art on the front.

Meanwhile, I had recently landed a clerical job at a law firm. One of the senior partners, Alec Bayless, came into the office one day, and I could see he was in a fair amount of pain. He was holding one of his hands up to a very swollen cheek.

"Hello, Brian," he mumbled.

"Alec, what happened?"

"I had some dental surgery, and an infection has set in. I'm going to have to cancel our family's trip to Australia this week. We've been planning it for a year but I don't think I'm going to make it like this," he lamented.

"We need to do something about this," I told him. "I'm going to run up to Pike Place Market and get you some wheatgrass juice; I think it will really help." I had previously read Ann Wigmore's books on wheatgrass and knew from personal experience of the amazing healing capabilities it contains. So I caught a bus to Pike Place Market, stopped by a juice bar I frequented, bought a few ounces to go, and took some of the moist, green pulp with me in a plastic baggie back to the law firm.

"Sip this juice slowly," Alec, I coached him. "Swirl it around in your mouth a bit. Good. Okay, now put some of this pulp between your check and gum and let it stay there a while. Oh, and the first thing you should know about drinking wheatgrass juice is that you'd better be close to a bathroom when you do. It has an immediate cleansing effect, if you know what I mean."

Seconds later, after taking a few cautious sips and putting the pulp inside his mouth, Alec was walking quickly toward the bathroom as if on cue. By the next day, the swelling in his cheek and jaw had almost completely disappeared, and Alec was able to embark on a major vacation with his family to Australia. Amazed with how my efforts had worked with Alec's situation, I felt that my future was going to be in the field of natural health. I knew there had to be some further purpose for me other than waking up each morning to face lawsuits every day. That sort of existence just didn't feel like a good fit for me anymore.

While performing my due diligence, which consisted of reading ads in some New Age magazines, I found that some schools and centers offered interesting graduate programs. One particular outfit looked impressive and honorable, but I didn't know if life under their Buddhist-oriented program would work for me. I respected the Buddha's work, but I just didn't know if I could handle giving myself completely over to it. Their program also came with a higher price tag than I was prepared to pay. A university near San Francisco had a transpersonal psychology program which looked quite good, but that was in a high-cost location and it was soon out of the running.

I then turned my attention to the ashram with the guru from the Himalayas, content knowing that they taught the classical yogic philosophy and traditions that I admired. India had produced some deep wisdom and great souls for thousands of years—I wanted to immerse myself in training that combined the tried and true with modern medical and psychological approaches, and the holistic yoga ashram offered that. They were also relatively affordable and vegetarian, so I filled out the application for their residential master's degree, the most comprehensive program they offered.

While waiting to hear back from them I tried a hatha yoga class with an expert from India who trained with B.K.S. Iyengar. At the class the instructor put us through a session from hell. Do you remember the soup-Nazi from *Seinfeld?* Well, this instructor was the Seinfeld soup-Nazi of yoga. *"Your arm is out of alignment! No yoga for you!"* My body was not prepared for holding perfectly aligned postures, and my ego took a beating from his scolding. I thought yoga was supposed to be peaceful and loving but apparently I had not been hearing the full story.

An acceptance letter came from the holistic yoga center in a few weeks, and I packed my gear and hit the road. I still had some time to head to Florida to visit Dad, where he was living now, and play at the tennis club he had joined there. He and his wife were fixtures there, along with many of the retired seniors in the planned community.

The extreme heat in Florida didn't bother me. Playing tennis in a sauna would even work for me. And that's what playing in Florida felt like. Upon arrival I saw that the club members were living my dream, playing every day on nice clay and grass courts, being coached by tanned professionals, and watching top pros at tournaments nearby.

The club members agonized over every aspect of their game, their equipment, and every point they played. Dad lined up a full schedule of doubles matches for us in the mornings and afternoons. He knew I was serious trouble for the old timers he played with; and when I visited, it was his best chance to rack up a string of wins. I was sandbagging a little bit with his 3.5 NTRP-level buddies, but I held back enough to make the matches interesting and fun. I was probably hitting about 5.0.

"No malice intended" was one of my old man's favorite lines after hitting a winner with extra force that either hit or came close to someone on the other team if they weren't able to move out of the way. He said it in a joking, apologetic voice and never meant any harm. This was his soft side and it was nice to see that he still had one.

Jim Courier came by the club a few times to hit with some of the teaching pros who worked there under the guidance of head pro, Tom Gullickson, brother of Tim, who had coached Pete Sampras. Tom had won a mixed-doubles title at Wimbledon with Manuela Maleeva in 1984. I sat at the courtside and admired Courier's strokes. When one of the pros couldn't make it to a doubles match from time to time, I was asked to fill in. As good as I thought I was, though, I could barely keep up with the power and the speed of their shots. If I was 6 inches taller and sixty pounds heavier I could have held my own but I was clearly the weakest link. Maybe tennis should have weight classes like boxing. The Maleeva sisters trained regularly at the club, and it was amazing to watch their workouts and consistency. I thought about asking them to play but then discarded that thought as it would have broken the flow of their workouts and could have been perceived as intrusive.

If the tennis club in Florida were ancient India, the bottom of the caste system at the club would have been the group of geriatrics called the Nooners. They were barely clinging to life and their state-of-the-art rackets. For some inhumane reason, the club scheduled them to play at noon, the hottest time of the day with direct overhead sun, when no one else was foolish enough to be out there. Some of the Nooners were nearly fossilized and could hardly move their legs more than a few steps, but they loved the sport with all their heart and were determined to play even if it killed them. They played horribly but they were willing to risk everything just to get out there and enjoy tennis one more hour—to hit the ball in the sweet spot just one more time. *God, how I loved these people!* They had such a pure love of the game that they inspired me more than anything. And so I joined them each day at noon and spent time practicing with them when nobody else would. I loved helping them work on their game and watch them swing at the ball in garish neon outfits that even Andre Agassi in his long-haired days would have thought twice about wearing.

"That's it," I encouraged them, doling out the very same instructions my father had given to me. "Get your racket back early! Keep your eye on the ball all the way into the racket!"

Others at the club invited me to play from time to time, and when I headed out to join an elderly gentleman on the court one day for doubles, the receptionist at the club asked me to come over and check in before going out to the court. I went to the desk, and one of the club pros walked over to me. Something was up.

"Brian, good morning! Have you paid for your court today?" the pro asked me.

"No, I thought I was covered under my father's plan."

"No, I'm sorry, his membership doesn't cover you. He receives guest passes each year and you can use one of those or pay cash."

"I don't have one, so I'll just go ahead and pay cash for today. Sorry for the misunderstanding."

Dad and I knew that he had been sneaking me into the club without paying the guest fees. He was still living with a Great Depression, there's-not-enough-to-go-around mentality and expected me to go along with that plan. Being ousted as a cheater was a major embarrassment for me. At its core, tennis is a moral game. But I was now exposed as someone in the tennis community who had violated one of the main ethical rules of tennis before I even stepped onto the court: Thou Shall Not Cheat. Shamed, I stayed away from the courts while word about the incident spread. When the urge to play eventually overcame my shame, I asked Dad for a guest ticket. He told me, "No, Brian, I can't give you one. We are saving those for someone who is coming to visit us after you leave."

Uh, excuse me. Was I not the Richie Tenenbaum of this family? Who could possibly love the game more than me? Who could possibly rate higher than I did for a guest pass? How could he do this to his own son, his best tennis buddy?

As it turned out, a few of his wife's relatives were going to be visiting. *But they barely knew how to play!* I thought. I was stunned and didn't say a word. I had always believed that tennis was the bond that held together my relationship with my father. I thought it would always be that way, but apparently things had shifted. The change felt irreversible so I didn't fight it. Maybe I shouldn't have been telling his wife to leave him while she still had some sanity left. She must have said something to him.

"But I love him, Brian. And he loves you, too. I know he does," she told me.

"He doesn't know what love is," I said with finality. She was trapped, and I could see that she would be with him until the end. The rest of us had barely escaped but she had nowhere else to go. I felt sorry for her and without Dad knowing, I taught his wife to drive his car so that one day she could perhaps gain just a little independence from him; so that she could drive herself to the tennis club and to the grocery store after he would eventually be too old to drive.

My stay with them came to an end and I took off for the yoga ashram, which was in another state. I had seen two tennis courts in their brochure so I had a good feeling about the place.

CHAPTER 9

Becoming a Holistic Yogi

One of my college friends, George, had grown up in a working-class town about an hour away from the ashram I was headed for. George's brothers, who still lived there, made sure I enjoyed my last few days of having the freedom to drink beer. They made sure we stopped at every bar in town. The area was not what you would call yoga country. It's Robert De Niro and Christopher Walken's *Deer Hunter* country, and they would most likely laugh or perhaps even throw you out of the restaurant or bar if you asked for a tofu burger. My hosts kindly put up with me until it was time to take me with my minor hangover to the bus station.

The bus dropped me off at a small town close to the ashram, and one of the staff members drove down to give me a lift. I entered the main lobby and approached the kind-looking receptionist with a nametag that read Mirra. She was about my parent's age and had a genuine smile that made me feel welcome.

"Good evening, looks like you are just arriving," said Mirra.

"Yes, my name is Brian Cox. I'm a new student in the program in Eastern studies."

"If you wouldn't mind filling out this paperwork, I can get you registered. Where are you from?"

"Out West, but I was just nearby with some friends for a few days."

"Oh, that's nice. Do they attend any of the courses here?" she asked.

Imagining how weird my beer-drinking, deer-shooting friends would find yoga, I answered, "No, they have other interests," and hoped she didn't ask what they were. Looking eternally hopeful, Mirra responded with a smile and said, "Well, maybe someday!"

The orientation booklet she handed me spelled out the rules at my new home: No alcohol, no illegal drugs, no romantic relationships, and no sex. Okay, so it was going to be another hardship post, but quite different than the ones I had been used to. Mirra gave me my room number and a few instructions. I headed down the hall with my suitcase and tennis racket. As I checked out the building I saw the two tennis courts and a basketball backboard outside. The cafeteria was down the hall on the left. The administrative offices and housing wing were down another long hallway. The women stayed on the top floor and the men on the ground floor. The doors to our rooms had no locks on them.

On the second floor at the end of the building, there was a group meditation room where everyone was supposed to gather at 10 o'clock each night to sing *bhajans*, which are Sanskrit devotional songs, and attend a group meditation. Sorry, but that is past my bedtime, and I'm not really into devotional chanting. I knew I was going to have trouble with that part of the program.

Sure enough, after a few nights of not showing up for the group meditations, one of the senior staff members asked me to come to his office.

"Come on in and have a seat, Brian."

"Sure, thanks."

"I just wanted to let you know that we've been missing you at the evening meditation sessions. They are part of your program and you really need to attend those."

"Yeah, I know. I didn't want to show up late so I just meditate in my room," which was at least a partial truth.

"The group meditations are pretty important, so if you could make those a part of your practice, you'll find it gets easier, okay?"

"Yes, of course," I agreed, but still feeling resistant.

I was too embarrassed to admit that I didn't really understand how to meditate and, to make matters worse, I couldn't sing worth a damn and didn't really care for the devotional *bhajans*. Beyond that, no matter how many pillows I sat on or how I positioned my legs, my body was not used to this type of sitting practice. I could not find any peaceful state or higher consciousness. But there was no way out of it. All of this was being supported by student loans with interest rates. So I followed everyone up the stairs at 10 o'clock each night and fidgeted through the group meditation with my knees aching, never getting anywhere near *samadhi* or enlightenment.

The bathrooms and stalls in the main building were lined with slabs of gorgeous Italian marble. Nice touch. It was a comfort that wannabe yogis like me who were renouncing the world could relieve themselves in style. As part of my karma-yoga contribution of eight hours of service per week, I was assigned to clean the bathrooms next to the carpeted auditorium.

Inside the main building there was also a full-service kitchen, a bakery, and a dining room. Breakfasts were oatmeal, bread, fruit, and sometimes scrambled tofu. Every Sunday, silence was observed in the dining hall; but almost without fail, a guest or resident would forget and utter just a few words until they realized why everyone was staring at them without responding. The guru had meals especially prepared for him by certain cooks who knew how to make authentic Indian cuisine. His meals were delivered to him in his private apartment in the main building. A core group of people dedicated to the guru lived in their own houses on the grounds as permanent staff. Some lived off the grounds. The publishing and mail-order operation was housed in a large barn with pallets of books being readied for shipment.

One day I noticed the guru walking down the hall carrying a tennis racket, dressed to play. A gaggle of American women wearing Indian saris followed him past the cafeteria and went outside. John, one of the residents who was sitting in the cafeteria, excused himself and joined the guru outside for a session of tennis. Everyone was welcome to watch, and it was quite a treat for some people whenever the guru came out and joined them.

Guruji, as they fondly called him, appeared to be in his 60s and was somewhat reclusive. He lived at his other ashram in India part of the year, on the banks of the Ganges River. Because of his fleeting presence, everyone wanted to be near him as much as possible when he stayed at the ashram. He was a large man; he stood six-feet tall and must have weighed over 200 pounds. Despite his girth, he moved well on court, and his strokes were confident and consistent. From the looks of his game he had obviously played a fair amount. John had excellent strokes, but his weakened body—he was at the center for health reasons—couldn't handle a strenuous workout. After a short while, they had to stop playing for John's sake.

Later that week when I was eating lunch in the cafeteria, a staff member approached me and asked if I would be able to play some tennis with Guruji. Apparently they had seen me out on the courts with some of the other residents. I told them I would be glad to play and gathered my gear. Another guest joined Guruji on his side, and we began hitting. When the big guru approached the net a few times, I cracked some shots past him and lobbed some over him, making it interesting for his partner to have to cover. After the guru came to the net a few more times, I passed him some more, and then I noticed the small crowd on the sideline whispering. *They must be impressed with my shots*, I thought to myself.

Then one of the courtside entourage walked up to me and informed me that the purpose of the session was to hit shots only to the Guruji so that he could practice and get a workout. I was not supposed to hit to the other person on the guru's side. Everyone was soon at ease as I fed their spiritual guide some easy shots and overheads at the net.

Against John, Guruji was used to swatting most shots away as winners, but my speed and anticipation kept the ball in play much longer. I could see he enjoyed our long rallies. Each time we played, I increased the speed of my strokes just a little to incrementally improve his game. When he was at the net, he loved to strike the ball with full force, and I worked on my form and defense until he needed a rest or some water. He nodded to me when it was time to either hit again or stop.

One afternoon after we played, Guruji walked over to chat with his admirers and I went with him. He went silent for a moment and perked up his head. Then, he turned and announced that a particular well-known swami had just been reborn that moment. I recognized the name and face for a split-second, and then the entourage walked away, everyone pleased to hear the news.

The guru and I continued our tennis workouts in the carpeted auditorium during the winter months. There were no marked lines, but we weren't there to play matches. I was there to be his silent coach and take his game to the next level. I saw his game and conditioning improve each time we played. As another part of my required karma-yoga contribution, I helped build the upstairs apartment where he lived out his final years. I hoped to get closer to him so I could learn any pearls of wisdom that were not in his books. But each day went by and Guruji never had any personal words for me.

Some guests came to the ashram for a weekend and ended up staying for months, and sometimes years. There was always a constant stream of spiritual seekers. This was my first glimpse into the lives of the subculture of the spiritual seekers who had left their former lives and even their families to chase God, gurus, and soulmates, and hopefully find some place to be accepted. They seemed like nice people, but I'm not like them, I thought to myself. I'm not spiritually confused or addicted...I'm just passing through.

Right behind searching for spiritual knowledge, looking for a soulmate seemed to be a favorite pastime for many seekers. This made forbidden love at the center and other ashrams even more exciting for those who dared. I imagined how much fun it would be to go on an extended ashram tour and check out the various retreats. A road trip like that would be a blast, looking for the most enlightened teacher, the perfect veggie burger, and maybe even finding that elusive soulmate or twin flame. The "twin flame" concept was taking metaphysical people by storm. The story seemed to go that soulmates were fulfilling an agreement to work on a karmic contract through their being together, while twin flames were far more in tune with each other's energy. These were the more challenging relationships as the reflection provided by the mirror of the other person involved was more obvious and direct.

Looking into what other ashrams had to offer, I learned about a similar yoga group in New England. They had their own guru and a nice catalog with smiling women in form-fitting yoga clothes. I didn't call to see if they had a tennis court or not, but the New England ashram was now high on my list. There were also the very low-budget ashrams. Jerry, one of my friends at the center, took me to visit one about thirty miles away. We pulled into their camp and Swami Jodie came out to greet us. Jerry said that nobody knew if Jodie was a man or woman but it really didn't matter to any of us. We were there for things of the spirit, not of the flesh. It was rainy and cold that day, and the residents welcomed us in for coffee, happy to have any visitors from the outside world. Once you landed in an ashram like this and had no transportation and little money, there was little hope of escape. It was the end of the line, the last stop on the budget-ashram tour for those who had nowhere else to go—a place I didn't want to end up. But, at least it existed for those who needed it.

If anyone was really serious about being a seeker and had the resources, there were more ashrams to choose from in India that were sponsored by various gurus. From what I could tell during dinner conversations, attending those was considered a badge of honor. There were also a few communes and spiritual groups on the West Coast, so becoming a seeker could actually become a lifelong adventure. The one big problem I noticed, however, was that there seemed to be plenty of seekers but not many finders. Well, I guess I had made my spiritual futon, and now I had to sleep on it at least for the next two years.

On many evenings after dinner, the students in our program were taught by a staff of doctors, psychologists, and philosophers who were also students of Guruji. The guru never taught our small group of students in the graduate program, although we heard him speak a few times at larger weekend gatherings where the public could attend. He stuck to the basic yogic teachings. The philosophy instructor informed us that the deepest teachings were ultimately taught from guru to student in silence. I asked him what tradition the guru's lineage had come from and he said, "It is called 'Hiranya-garbha,' The Golden Womb." The tradition is closely related to the one headed by the Maharishi Mahesh Yogi, who the Beatles had visited in India, to learn meditation.

Even though I had read a few books and had attended a hatha class in preparation, I was just starting my formal practice and study of the entire system of yoga, so I began with the fundamentals. In our classes, I soon learned that the foremost authority on yoga was the sage Patanjali. He was the author of *The Yoga Sutras*, the definitive book on yoga, which he produced around the year 200 BCE. The goal of the book was to describe the methods of attaining self-realization, with each chapter going into further detail. The first sutra says that yoga, or union, was achieved by controlling the "modifications of the mind."

To help us meditate we learned the "*so-hum*" technique of focusing the mind on this Sanskrit word…"*so*" on the inhale and "*hum*" on the exhale. Those two words mean "I am that," and with each inhalation and exhalation, the practitioner affirms their oneness with all that exists.

Our instructors described the *yamas* and *niyamas* of yoga as the ethical and moral guidelines in yoga. Mastery over the *yamas* and *niyamas* is said to bring good karmic fruits and allow one to work intensely on the next step higher on the ladder. The *yamas* include not harming, not lying, not stealing, not wasting, and not accumulating possessions. The first *niyama* is purity, which gives indifference to the body. The second combines happiness and mental clarity. The third is contentment, which gives pleasure and comfort. The fourth is austerity, which creates desire for growth and the perfection of the body and senses. The fifth is self-study, which creates the appearance of the chosen deity within the mind. And the final one is surrender to the ultimate reality, which results in *samadhi*, a one-pointed state of consciousness where only consciousness is experienced.

Asanas, we were taught, when practiced as effortless physical postures, help people transcend the pairs of opposites that create suffering, such as the concepts of good and evil, pleasure and pain, or even hot and cold. *Asanas* help practitioners to relax and focus on the infinite. I was pleased with the ashram's style of gentle yoga that focused on awareness. Keep that Iyengar stuff away from me!

Pranayama breathing exercises are said to expand the field of *prana*, or vital energy, from all sides and seek to purify and bring practitioners into balance with the external world. I knew I had to be careful with the breathing exercises, as I didn't feel comfortable pushing things too far, too fast.

Pratyahara, control of the senses by relaxation, was described as bringing the mind back to its own seat from sensory involvement with the external world. The inner connection from one lower rung on the ladder of yoga to the higher levels is established when the mind is able to stay in its own nature while focused on an object of concentration. *Dharana*, concentration is the next level, where the mind is trained to focus on one object, such as a mantra.

The state of *dhyana*, or meditation, is when the mind is one-pointed in an uninterrupted flow. The concept of *dhyana* emerged from yogic teachings, and traveled north into China where it evolved into Chan Buddhism. Then the teachings morphed into Zen when the concepts moved to Japan. The word *dhyana* is believed to be associated with *The Book of Dyzan* that is mentioned in ancient wisdom and was used by Madame Blavatsky as a resource for her books and work that caused a sensation in the late 1800's.

The main philosophy instructor, who was perhaps the dearest student of Guruji, described a simple method of yogic meditation for us as follows: sit with the spine erect, and then begin to observe the thoughts in the mind. Let the thoughts flow by like a river without getting attached to them. One side of the river is the material world, and on the other side sits God. When the thoughts are of the limited and impermanent material world, bring the thoughts back to the eternal aspect, God. Doing this establishes new grooves in the riverbed of the mind closer to the side of the riverbank that God is on. Now that I had committed to following a spiritual path, I was ready to head for the river bank that God was on, and so I began practicing this method.

Samadhi, described as spiritual absorption with the supreme consciousness, is the ultimate step where all fluctuations of the mind have been dissolved. The state of awareness known as *samadhi* takes a yogi up to, but not into, the state called *turiya*, which is the conscious combination of the waking, dreaming, and sleeping states. There is a distinction between a lower and a higher *samadhi*. In the lower *samadhi*, thought constructs within the mind still exist, like the steppingstones used to cross a stream.

As a yogi progresses through the stages of the lower, he or she leaves the previous stages behind and they dissolve. It is said that when he reaches the last stage of lower *samadhi*, the *dharma-mega*—the cloud of virtue—overcomes the bad karma of an individual. In that clear level of awareness, the good karmic patterns destroy themselves after they kill the bad ones, leaving one's duties fulfilled. Then one is said to become a *jivan mukta*, one who is liberated in this present life.

This is the transition to higher *samadhi* where consciousness exists in its own nature as pure light. *Samyama* is a combined state of concentration, meditation, and *samadhi*. This level of awareness allows one to see the uniqueness of an object, into its intrinsic nature. In this state of being, one understands the true condition by tuning into a single moment during the transformation that occurs when change takes place. Being able to know the past and the future comes because the mind becomes able to experience time as a unified field of existence. *Samyama* on the concept of slow and quick fruition gives knowledge of death and approaching evil. *Samyama* on friendship gives power and strength. *Samyama* on the ear and in the space is said to bring divine hearing, known as clairaudience. *Samyama* on the body and in the space causes the body to turn into light. *Aha*, now I knew I was on the right track! The yogis knew all about the mysteries of higher consciousness and about the subtle light of the body. *Yep! This was exactly the information I had been looking for!*

The sutras of Patanjali also describe how to acquire supernormal powers, called *siddhis*, which accompany spiritual growth through the practice of yoga. They include mastery over the elements, the ability to become invisible, the ability to become as small as the smallest atom or as large as the universe, to levitate, and to have God-consciousness and aid evolution. Seekers are warned, however, that the *siddhis*, when pursued for self-interest, are impediments to the ultimate knowledge of God and are best left alone. It was comforting to learn in-depth how the ancients described their experiences of higher consciousness and that there was a definite method to achieve it. I also learned that awakening the *kundalini* energy within the body was a dangerous method to achieve higher consciousness and that it is better left alone; let nature take its course.

In each course within our program, we engaged in self-reflective and experiential work. The projects we undertook were experiments and observations about ourselves, so that we became more aware of how our inner states worked in relation to our outer personalities, emotions, and physical bodies. We learned and practiced a variety of mind and body techniques for stress management and optimal performance of body and mind, like proper diaphragmatic breathing and guided relaxation. We practiced two-to-one breathing, which oxygenates the body more efficiently by taking twice as long to exhale as it does to inhale.

The training in psychotherapy included learning and practicing Hakomi, a body-centered therapy based on the key principles of mindfulness, nonviolence, organicity, unity, and body-mind holism. Organicity means that the body and mind have the capacity for self-healing. It was fascinating when one of our instructors led us through an introductory Hakomi technique and we got our first, small taste of it. First, he had us relax in our seats, then he guided us, "Close your eyes, and go into a state of mindfulness." Then he said the following words calmly and in a friendly voice as a thought probe, so that we could observe our internal response to it: "You are perfectly welcome here." We let the probe sink in, and the thoughts and realizations that came to me immediately were, *What a nice thing to hear! I never felt totally welcome in our house when I was growing up and it was because of my father. There is also a part of me that doesn't feel welcome in the world.*

Some of the most memorable times for me at the Ashram were the evenings we spent listening to the stories of the ancient sages shared by the philosophy instructor from India. When I watched him lecture to large groups in the auditorium, as he became more passionate about a subject, I allowed my eyes to un-focus and I could see the subtle light-energy around his body increase in size and intensity against the dark background of the stage. As impressive as the stories about the sages were, I wanted to come into direct contact with great souls and experiences, like the ones he spoke about, and not just hear about them second-hand or read about them by myself in the cold, lonely library.

129

After a few months of morning hatha classes at 6 o'clock held in the chilly classrooms, we progressed to learning some of the cleansing techniques. We started with the Neti Pot, a ceramic container designed to rinse the nasal cavity; that was easy enough. Next it came time to perform the cleansing practices called "the upper wash and "the lower wash." At first those sounded interesting and rather harmless, perhaps even a little erotic—boy, was I wrong about that! The recommendation was to do the upper wash at the change of seasons to help the body adjust and release any cellular liquids and material that would otherwise end up coming out through a cold or runny nose.

To learn the upper wash, they marched us outside before breakfast on a brisk morning into a grassy area behind the building, where nobody else could see us. After all, witnessing half-a-dozen people throwing up early in the morning might shock some of the newer guests. Each of us carried a gallon jar of warm salt water that we had just mixed up. We milled around on the frosty grass, half asleep, receiving last-minute instructions. The goal was to get as much of it down as quickly as possible. When we were ready, we began chugging like thirsty freshmen at a college keg party. There is really nothing that compares to swallowing nearly a gallon of salt water quickly except drowning in the ocean, I think. Do not attempt this without professional supervision.

Before long, some of the other students began throwing up from the weight of the water in their stomachs. The rest of us held the water down the best we could and performed *udhiyana bhanda* and *nauli*, yogic stomach contractions to swish the water around and get a full cleansing. The coach then told us, "Get the remaining water out by sticking your finger down your throat to trigger the gag reflex. That's it. Get it all out. You don't want a lot of salt water left in your stomach."

We responded with more gagging and salty snot dripping out of our noses.

"There you go. Good job, guys! And don't eat much at breakfast; keep it very light," the coach warned.

I felt like my performance was adequate and that these types of practices might even feel normal to me someday. Then it was time to learn the lower wash and that was even trickier. For the lower wash to work properly, the recommendation was to perform a self-administered enema the night before. The next morning, not having eaten anything, we gathered in the briefing room. One of the staff members gave us final instructions. He wrote on the blackboard, "Pat don't rub." I didn't know who "Pat" was, but if "Pat" didn't rub, that was fine with me. Carts with hot water and sliced lemons were then wheeled in, and we began sipping the mixture, which was just about hot enough to burn our tongues. The water had to be hot enough to open the pyloric valve, bypass the urinary tract, go through the intestines, and then out the back door.

The coach warned us saying, "Don't let the water get much cooler, or the technique won't work properly. Then you'll have to start all over again." So we sipped and sipped, and waited. Before too long we each made a trip to the bathroom and then repeated the process. It was only after a few trips that I realized what "Pat don't rub" was all about. He had forgotten to use a comma after "Pat."

The most difficult cleansing technique by far was swallowing the *dhauti* cloth. I was actually the only person in the program willing to attempt this maneuver. Thankfully, my neighbor down the hall was a veteran of the technique. He came by one night to guide me through it, and I trusted his experience. In his day, Jerry had been a card dealer in Las Vegas, had been married seven times to various strippers, and claimed to know about the conspiracy behind the JFK assassination from being in a bar with Jack Ruby a few days before it happened. I was still going with the single-shooter theory, but Jerry was definitely my kind of yogi, devoted but a rebel at heart.

He cautioned me that on one occasion while doing the *dhauti* cloth maneuver he had swallowed about nine feet of his cloth, and had let it sit in his stomach too long. The cloth started to go further down into his system than it should have, and when he tried to pull it back up, it was stuck. He said it took several people to pull it back out. Hearing that didn't deter me but it did bring up a little extra fear. On my night of honor, I chose a finely woven cloth strip, medical grade, about two inches wide. Jerry brought an old one of his as a backup. He placed a small bowl of water in front of me and we soaked the cloth in it.

"How do you feel, man?" he asked.

"Yeah, I've been fasting. My stomach is empty and I feel ready."

"Don't worry. We'll get you through with flying colors."

"Just keep an eye on the time."

"Dip the cloth in the water and ball up the end of it. Not too big. There, that's enough. Put it toward the back of your throat. That makes it easier to start swallowing."

I nodded and did as he directed. After the first few swallows, I began to realize that this process was going to take a fair amount of time, so I started swallowing more quickly.

"Go slowly! You don't want to throw it up and have to start over." he cautioned.

Overcoming the sense and fear of suffocation was part of the experience, so I got a chance to face my death issues as the cloth went down. After getting most of the cloth down and into my stomach and still holding onto the end that was sticking out of my mouth, I performed several abdominal muscle contractions, to help the cloth clean my inner stomach lining.

When Jerry motioned, I slowly pulled up the cloth. The cloth was coated in stomach acid, which burned my throat just a bit, and I put it in the bowl to wash it later. When it was all over, he smiled at me and said, "Hey, you did great!" We went back to our respective rooms and meditated, and I fell asleep feeling proud about being more of a real yogi than ever.

My mother and Bob Johnson hug at their wedding in Cairo

The secret Lobsang Rampa Fan Club at the ashram with
my yogic mentor Jerry (Credit – Jim Ingram)

Getting ready to leave the ashram for the West
Coast with friend Jim Ingram

CHAPTER 10

A Jungian Astrologer and an Osteopath

In the psychology courses, I learned that Sigmund Freud's protégé, Carl Jung, had a strong interest in Eastern philosophy and spirituality. And having had an interest in astrology since childhood, I felt it was time to have a professional look over my chart to give me some feedback in a way that reflected Jung's understandings. Fortunately, New York City was only a few hours away from Scranton by bus. Once I located a Jungian astrologer there, I provided him with my date and time of birth and he prepared my chart. I then caught the bus to New York and, after a short subway trip, found his apartment. I knocked on the door, and was greeted by Julian. He was a slight, bookish man most likely in his 60s, who wore glasses and had a gentle manner. We sat down and, after some small talk, Julian began.

"Scorpios are a fixed sign," he said. "They get into a place and stay there. They tend to hold on emotionally and don't let go of things. If they have broken romances or if there are problems with their parents or siblings or friends, they hold onto the hurt. They get a certain amount of pleasure out of making themselves miserable. Aries, for example, would blow up over something in a moment of anger and a whole spurt of fire would arise, but in a half-hour it would be over. Not so for Scorpio. Two years later, he'll still be thinking about the incident. Air-sign people have a capacity to be detached; they can look at themselves as they would look at an outer object. Water sign people, and Scorpios especially, do not have this capacity. The best way to work at it is to think of it from the perspective of other people. With the lack of air and lots of water,

135

one of the major things you have to live with and try to handle is finding a way of having some detachment. The danger of hanging on to anger and hurt is that it becomes self-poison."

I reflected for a moment, then I asked him, "What do you recommend?"

"Do you know Joseph Campbell's work in mythology?"

"I've seen his name in bookstores, but haven't read any of his books."

"I would think mythology would be something you would be absolutely gaga about. Any mythology would help, but Campbell wrote a very useful book you might try, *A Hero with a Thousand Faces.* I suggest you look at Campbell and mythology because myths are dramatic stories. They are stories of hands-on experience. Icarus flies too close to the sun, his wings of wax melt, and he falls to the earth.

"There is not one word of rational explanation in it. Campbell has the capacity to read myths and interpret myths, and see the broader meaning. He relates them from one culture to another, and finds the underlying mythic beliefs common to all cultures. There are different names for different Gods, and the stories are slightly different here and there, according to culture. They are like fairy tales. I think that your interest in psychology would make Jung interesting to you, and Campbell wrote *The Portable Jung.* This will combine the intellectual needs of what you are doing with your imaginative and experiential needs.

"Saturn has a real inhibiting effect on Mars, which can produce a lot of frustration, a lot of anger. Saturn can also provide the structure, the form, the discipline which Mars really needs. Mars, pure and simple, has no direction. Any direction is okay. It has no carry-through. There is a double message here: On one hand, there is a lot of anger and frustration in the chart, a lot of feeling that you are not allowed to do what you want to do. A lot of 'I'm going to be who I'm going to be. I'm going to do what I want to do.' But, it's also a square, and the sun can represent authority figures. Uranus is in the first house. So, 'I want to do what I want to do' is in conflict with an authority figure. If this chart is right on the button, not more than 10 minutes wrong, then it is very likely that the authority figure is a father figure, probably *your* father. There is a lot of conflict with a paternalistic figure who says 'you can't.'"

I had a feeling this topic would come up during the reading. "Yep, that would be my father," I remarked.

"Saturn is the father figure who lays down the law. Mars is the 14-year-old who rightly rebels because you can't become a person unless you rebel, unless you break away from your parents and become somebody," Julian continued while studying the chart. "You are 27 years old and coming into what is called the 'Saturn return.' The general experience people have from maybe two years before to two years after, more or less, is a lot of shaking and changing with jobs and careers, insecurity, not knowing where you are going. And what you find out when you are about 32 years old is that you look at yourself as you were at the age of 25 or 26 and you realize you have grown up. Now, it is impossible at the age of 25 to think that you have grown up. You have grown up physically, but there is a maturation that comes with the Saturn return."

Julian continued, "You kind of say to yourself, 'Wait a minute—I really might live to be 45 or even 60, and I better have some money in the bank...I should get that union card.' One has the feeling that one is about to make a commitment, and you are not quite sure what to make the commitment to."

I knew exactly what he was describing. "What else can you see?" I asked as he took the chart in his hands.

"There is a strain with the strong Uranian nature and the strong Saturn stuff in your chart in your first house. You want to be free and independent, and then there is this very strong tension involving the 'rules of the game' you must play by. This brings you a lot of tension with your inner father figure. The authority figure seems to be saying, 'You must do such and such.' Life is a matter of living through this process. One takes the authority figure of Saturn, internalizes it, and you yourself choose to go to bed early to get up early so that you can go to the job you have, so you can go to night school. It is no longer wicked, old, nasty Dad saying you have to do your homework. It is something you have made part of yourself. The process is never completely done.

If you are lucky, most of it is done by the end of your second Saturn return at age 60."

Julian continued with some astrological progressions and said "your chart indicates the possibility of enough suffering to become a good therapist one day."

If he only knew! We concluded the session and I thanked Julian for his work and headed down on the elevator. On the bus back to the ashram, I realized that I was not going to be able to really help anyone or even myself therapeutically until I resolved the issues I still had with my old man.

***

An osteopathic physician from New York City attended a few courses with us at the holistic center. At the time, my physical body also needed some attention and repair; I was looking for a way to heal a severe sprain on my left ankle. Playing slam-dunk basketball in the snow on the court I had set up at the ashram was probably not the wisest move. The physician invited me to New York City to be one of his first patients, so one day I signed out from the holistic center and went for an appointment. He was a specialist in cranial manipulation and homeopathy.

The initial consultation consisted of measuring my range of movement and then him asking me many questions that other doctors had never asked me, like, "Does your body tend to seek warmth or coolness? Do you get up in the morning early, or do you sleep in late?" He listened to my answers and took careful notes. Then came more questions about my various personality traits and habits. The questions were designed to help him learn about my particular constitution so he could select the proper remedy. He had me stand up and checked the range of motion and strength-resistance of each arm and leg, again jotting down the results. Then it was up onto the treatment table. His attention came to my swollen ankle, which was one of the problems I wanted him to look at. I had landed wrong on it foolishly playing basketball on the icy outdoor court.

The doctor gently put his hands under my ankle and held it gently. Instead of forcing the ankle like I would have normally, he allowed the ankle and foot to rest in his hands and feel supported. I observed how he let the ankle and foot move ever so slightly in the manner and direction in which it felt most comfortable going. The range of motion slowly increased without any effort or pain. It was amazing to watch and feel what he was doing, because it was all so very subtle. He said, "This type of treatment allows the ankle to trust us by letting it do what it wants to do, and move how it wants to be moved, and by not forcing it." It was a revelation to me. Most of what I had learned from my father all my life had been how to forcefully tear down people and things until they broke—physically, mentally, and emotionally.

With homeopathy, which was my next form of treatment, the doctor explained that the practitioner ideally prescribes one remedy for all of the combined symptoms, not the mixed remedies you purchase at health-food stores. Since there is no measurable amount of the actual substance used in its final form, the remedy works on the subtle energies of the body that in turn influence the physical.

To select the proper remedy, he had me lie on my back with my eyes closed. Then he placed his hands under my head and sensed the pulse of the cranial-sacral fluid. His assistant placed a single vial of tincture in my outstretched hand while the doctor felt the effect of the remedy on the pulse near the base of my skull. She did not tell the doctor or me which one she had placed in my hand so that neither of us would be influenced by knowing. The rhythm of the cranial-sacral fluid was sensitive to each remedy, and his fingertips picked up on the almost imperceptible fluctuations of the pulse caused by each one. Using this method, he was absolutely certain which remedy was the best for me.

Then he performed a cranial manipulation on me. The movement of his fingers on my skull was so subtle I didn't feel that anything was being done. However, he said, "There are some pieces moving out of alignment that if untreated will affect the rest of your body over time." He used his soft hands to guide the skull plates toward a better position. My friend was a true wizard of healing, and I was honored to be one of his first clients. After the treatment I left the hustle and bustle of New

York and headed back to the calm, quiet ashram. I hoped that someday I would be able to assist other people like the fine osteopath had done for me.

Having completed my final courses and finding that life in the ashram was no longer a good fit for me, I got ready to leave on a cross-country road trip with Jim Ingram. Jim was a temporary resident of the ashram who wanted to check out the West Coast. He had also lived overseas in the Middle East and South America, so with that in common, plus the fact that he had a rebellious streak like me, we became fast friends. While at the ashram, Jim had hung out at the secret pizza and non-alcoholic beer parties I threw during the NFL playoff games. No televisions were allowed for guests at the ashram, but Earl, the crusty old mechanic and groundskeeper had a small black and white set he let us watch in the garage, which was far enough away from the main building for anyone to see or hear us.

When it was time to leave, Jim and I said some goodbyes, jumped into his car, and we were on our way.

One night in Virginia on our way to a party we had been invited to by a former neighbor and dear friend of mine, Brenda, we pulled over and stopped for gas. A heavyset attendant with a grease-stained, one-piece blue uniform limped over to the car as I opened the door to get out. The limp looked oddly familiar. As he got closer and I could see his face, I could see that it was the boy my father had been a Big Brother to years ago! He was now a grown man, working as a gas station clerk.

We chatted for a few minutes and I told him that I would let Dad know we met. It was incredible to see that he was able to make his way in life this far, despite the massive amount of difficulty and hardships he had suffered growing up. Our tank was full and we had to leave, so I said goodbye and we pulled onto the freeway. As we drove away, I marveled at the synchronicity of seeing our old friend appear out of nowhere. Of all the gas stations we could have stopped at in Virginia, we ended up at that one. The spontaneous reunion felt like an auspicious sign. It was as if the unseen hand of the universe was showing me that no matter how strange it may have looked to anyone else, somehow I was heading in the right direction. But I knew that I would have to see quite a few more obvious signs, and hopefully some much bigger ones down the road just to make sure.

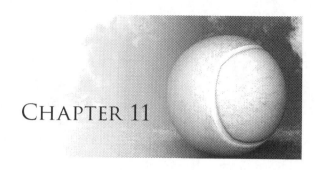

CHAPTER 11

Message from the Other Side

Jim and I drove to the West Coast along a southern route and then went north from California into Oregon. The landscape shifted from desert browns into misty, green mountains. Then came the farmlands of Central Oregon and the Willamette Valley. Armed full of knowledge about holistic health, yoga, and meditation but somewhat short on actual experience, I arrived in the Pacific Northwest without a clue as to what I would do next. After going through a recent divorce, my sister had an extra room in her house, so she rented it to me while I looked for work. Her two teenage sons, also lived in the house with her. I had known them since birth, and we all got along quite well.

My friend Jim found the Northwest to his liking as I had suspected he would. He found an apartment in the area and pursued his outdoor photography business, hiring a college buddy who now had U.S. Army Special Forces experience, and therefore was the perfect companion for Jim so that he could go into the remote Alaskan wilderness and other exotic locales to capture those priceless shots.

Not wanting to end up in another cubicle job, I looked through the classifieds to see if I could find a position that matched my qualifications: vegetarian yoga therapist, cosmic philosopher, and major tennis and Ping-Pong geek. Nothing really jumped off the page, but I wasn't giving up hope. After all, the Harmonic Convergence had only happened the previous year, in 1987. The Convergence was a global meditation, the first of its kind, done in alignment with planetary positions and the

Mayan calendar. Perhaps my timing was a tad early for the New Age job market that I was imagining.

A few weeks later I looked in another edition of the Sunday paper and lo and behold, there it was: an ad for meditation instructors at a place called the Meditation Station. Yes! I thought, *This is it! My timing was perfect all along.* I could now imagine a future working in meditation and yoga franchises all across America. Customers would be lined up out the door to learn the upper and lower wash. *There you go. Step right up. Pat, don't rub. You folks doing the upper wash, throw up over there.* It didn't matter to me that I didn't really meditate or do much hatha yoga; I knew how to teach it and it was time to get everyone else started.

I turned onto Pacific Highway 99 and located the address in a one-story office building next to the Cal Worthington car dealership. Pulling into the parking lot, I could see by the exterior of the building that there were probably no bathrooms with Italian marble inside like at the holistic yoga ashram. But that was okay. I was willing to settle for less for the right opportunity. I walked inside trying hard not to appear too enthusiastic or over confident. A pleasant lady greeted me.

"Good afternoon, can I help you?" she asked.

"Hi. My name is Brian and I stopped by because of the ad in the paper for meditation instructors. Can I leave my resume with you?"

"Sure! Please come in," I was told.

A door down the hall was open and I noticed a massage table set up in one of the rooms. *Great!* I thought. *This will be an excellent growth opportunity for me.*

"Is there anything else you need from me right now?" I asked.

"No, this will be fine. I'm sure Tracy will call you in the next few days."

I went home and looked forward to coming back for an interview where I would present my credentials and regale them with a few inside stories about the Swami and me. The next week, I was shocked to read in the news that the police had raided the Meditation Station. Holy Shiva! The place was a front for a tantric sex-oriented business that provided illegal sensual massages and related services. Well, what the Kali Yuga did I know? I was just a wandering sadhu fresh off the ashram.

My hopes were dashed and I ended up landing a cubicle job, the very thing I was hoping to avoid upon my return to so-called civilization. I was hired by a business that performed psychological analysis of job candidates and specialized in recruiting plumbers. Go figure. The psychologist at the firm, knew from our lunchtime discussions that I was seeking deeper insights about life and what path I should be following next. She referred me to her friend, Ruth, who did psychic readings. So I contacted Ruth, set a date for an appointment, and when the day arrived I took the ferry across Puget Sound to her home on Whidbey Island.

I knocked on the door and Ruth welcomed me into her home with a German accent. If I had to guess how old she was I would say that she was getting close to retirement age. After a brief introduction we walked into her living room. I sat down on the couch and she sat closely in front of me in a chair. She reached out for my hands and held them for a few moments.

"As I touch you, I go into your vibration and always see the psychic vision that is symbolic for you at this time in your life," she said.

"At first, I see you climbing a pole, peering out a lookout. Then I see you climbing stairs in a building. You are opening doors. The next picture is rather interesting. I see you opening windows. Everything is a lookout. Do you understand?"

I nodded my head and replied, "Yes, I've been seeking spiritual knowledge and understanding ever since I can remember."

She let go of my hands and remarked, "What I see is a symbol that you are in search of something. I've never seen that with anyone as much as with you. Every individual is different, but apparently you're actively looking for something and haven't found it."

"Yes, that's what I am going through," I said, still hoping for more specific guidance.

"You are striving to go higher, to put more challenge into your life. You're a person who always needs a challenge. You will easily get bored with working situations where you have to do the same thing every day. You need to strive higher still. So go into your venture in life, and remember that you hold your life in your own two hands. Nobody does but you. There is still so much ahead of you. I'm glad that you're climbing because you can really reach the top."

Ruth continued, "Our aura is like a big eggshell around us. By thinking of something nice or saying a prayer or listening to music, this eggshell opens and the colors flow gently out in beautiful vibrations around us. So you are slowly opening up. You are not quite sure yet. You are still a little skeptical. We will overcome that in a moment. Your yellow, your mind, is outstanding; it is the outstanding color in your aura. It shows me that you are an educated man; that you are striving for more education. You are not finished."

Ruth pointed her hand toward my throat and said, "There's a soft glow over your throat chakra, which shows me that you use it a lot. This chakra is very well developed. Here is your pink flowing out. Interestingly enough, the core is a very deep vibration of pink, and it comes out a little lighter and then it stops. That means you have built up a barrier, and there is one little crack in your heart. You had a bad experience with somebody that made you very alert, so you don't want to get hurt anymore. You are careful, and you are a little afraid of love."

"I was in love once and it didn't work out well," I said, thinking of Helene, a sweet girlfriend from my college days and how I had ruined that beautiful relationship. *Why do I want love so much and then push it away when I find it?* I couldn't figure that one out.

"Remember, Brian, you co-created that experience together. We come into this world, what I call 'Schoolhouse Earth', of our own free will. God gives us the heritage of free will, free choice, and free decision. Please keep that in your mind for the rest of your life. You came to experience life. So you can't stop it even if you have a bad experience. That doesn't mean you might not have 10 other bad ones if you choose. Don't be afraid. Go on with your life. Be open. Other people don't see auras, but they can sense them. If your heart energy is not flowing, nobody will come in. Do you understand?"

"Yes. But I'm not sure I'm willing to risk hurting someone else again," I confided.

"You need to open up, no matter what happens. You need to pray and use your good judgment to find the right one. You haven't found it yet. You are holding back and too afraid of letting go. If you are in love and everything is fine, your heart energy will flow and will be very vibrant. It's all right to love with the mind, too, but the heart is more important. If you want a good relationship, you need to let your love flow because it is giving and receiving. You have already encountered some hardships and suffering, and things have been difficult."

Thoughts of my father ran through my mind about how unappreciated he had made me feel. Ruth continued, "You struggled with a lot of things. But look, be honest with yourself, this was what made you who you are today. This is what I call inner strength. You have it. You got it through these experiences. It's all right. Let go of the suffering. Just don't make the same mistakes with others. These were all learning, life experiences, and many times we choose that. It's incredible why people hang onto hard things. Why? Let it go. Stuff it all into a garbage sack, mentally, and throw it in the river. See it float away. You don't need to sit on that stuff. Then recharge yourself. See yourself under a waterfall and feel cleansed. Let it swim away, and then new energy, positive energy, fills you. That's what makes life worthwhile, not hanging on to negative stuff."

Signaling to my lower torso, she said, "Here is a lot of brown. You need earth energy. That will help you balance yourself. Your greens are very faded. Green is the vibration of inner balance. Get those colors from nature, from creation. Go out and touch trees, touch the pine needles, absorb through the fingertips and absorb through the eyes. Cedar and pine are very helpful. Look very closely and you will see detail. It takes about seven or 10 minutes, and your inner eye will open. It should also be a moment when you say, 'Thank you, God, I can see again.' When you were little, you loved nature much more than you do now. You don't make time for nature anymore, but you need to. You need to lie on the ground this summer as often as possible, on the grass. Absorb the Earth's energy. Lie on your back for 10 minutes, then on your tummy. You will see what I mean. You need at least 15 minutes a day in a park. Go take a hike. Open yourself. Open your five senses. Recharge yourself. And, get in touch with God."

She paused and then said, "Your spiritual aura is just on the verge of coming out. The spiritual aura is naturally the true self. Everything else we leave behind. Do you realize this?"

"Are you talking about the soul?" I asked.

Ruth didn't answer my question directly but continued in her own train of thought, "When we step out of this body, the body is nothing. Our wonderful mind is nothing. But how we unfold spiritually, that is the true endeavor. We don't change over there on the other side. All those improvements we want to make, we have to make them here. This is why we are in the physical, material world. You can't learn this much up in the spirit world. It's a different experience, all right? So each time when we return to Earth, we choose to return for the simple reason to grow spiritually. It's called 'soul evolution.'

"Everything works as it is supposed to; otherwise, this planet wouldn't be here and the stars wouldn't be there." Ruth covered her mouth, coughed and said, "You have somebody with you. Whenever another vibration steps into the room…this is not the normal cough."

She coughed again to clear her throat and then spoke in a raspy voice. "This is a gentleman who is on the other side that I feel was family. You would understand. He's older. Not as young as you are. He's not a small man, and he is very tired, as if whatever happened… or, he was on medication before he died. He's giving me this feeling so you would understand who he is. It could be one of your grandfathers. He's taller and had good-sized shoulders. He's smiling at you. It's nice to make that contact. He is shaking his head. Tennis. In my inner vision, I see a tennis racket with you. That is also wonderful for you, especially your balance. If they show me a tennis racket, it's the right sport for you and you can also meet nice people."

Ruth continued, "Good luck, you can do it. Go on. Climb your mountain. Climb your stairs. Go on. That is what he is telling you."

I knew this was in reference to my search for self-realization and was glad to have Papa Cox's support from the other side.

"You are restricted but your inner core is beautiful. You are a loving, caring person and you deserve better. The universal law means giving and receiving. If it doesn't work, nothing works. Think about that. And if you are in that first state of exploring a relationship with somebody, it's a very important state. If you sense that somebody just can't be open enough to share and to give to you, then be cautious. If it is her personality, there is nothing you can do. You deserve better. You are the master of your life. I can only just tell you what I receive here.

There is a beautiful ray of deep violet around your heart. And that I like very much, so somehow you are working. Your sole desire, your sole purpose when you came back into this world was to be of service to mankind. And you will never be able to push that away. So you are doing it already, otherwise, I wouldn't see this. And that means you are very good in what you are doing. I'll tell you what kinds of people show these colors—they are nurses, doctors and counselors."

I thought the session was about to end but Ruth perked up and continued. "Now we have a young guy who is on the other side and wants to be remembered. Is there somebody who committed suicide? This is what I strongly pick up but it happened a while ago."

"There is only one person I knew who died that way. He was a friend from college."

Ruth went on. "I feel so touched I want to cry. He needs help. You need to pray for him. When you come home today will you get a candle, light a candle for him? I will help him, too. You see, he can't go on. He needs somebody to show him the way. He's stuck. I had a sister like that. And this is why I am involved in this work. Because somebody told me pretty much the same story I am telling you. And I know my sister is alright now but she was for 25 years in that void.

"She needed my forgiveness and I had forgotten. I'm glad you said his name because he really needs our help. He is approaching you. He needs to go on toward the light and that's what you need to say. 'Go find the light.'"

I spoke to my old friend as if I could see him, "Tim, go find the light."

Ruth continued, "But he needs a prayer from this side. Eventually he will have to return and do his whole lifetime over. And if you have people you counsel, you better make them aware of that."

We made our silent prayers to my friend. Then Ruth opened her eyes and I said to her, "I really appreciate what you've shared with me and what we just did."

"He will find his way. I can see that he is ready to go now."

It was now time to end the session. She stood up, walked me to the door, and we hugged goodbye.

Sitting in the ferry parking lot I watched the wind kick up white caps on Puget Sound and thought about my friend who had died and how glad I was that we were able to help him move on. Then my mind turned to the message I had just received during my session with Ruth, the one from Papa Cox. He was right. I needed to spend more time with the things I could always count on to bring me joy and make me feel glad to be alive: tennis and table tennis.

So my nephew, Dana, and I began practicing table tennis almost daily after Jean moved a table into the living room of her house in Federal Way. It felt great to pass on the traditional drills to Dana and his game picked up quickly. Then I learned there was a table tennis club with some USATT-rated players in Seattle that rolled out some quality tables a few nights a week in the gym at my alma mater. When it seemed like Dana was sufficiently prepared we went to watch and maybe even get some games in with some of the players.

Dana was too used to my style of play, and it was imperative for him to play against different people if he was going to improve. The level of play in the room was intimidating and I questioned whether I had made the right decision by coming. But the sound of celluloid balls bouncing on several tables and shoes squeaking on the hardwood floors was too much to resist. I approached a woman who looked to be in charge. She had tournament patches all over her jacket and was directing the operation.

"Hi, we just came to see if it was possible to play. Do you accept drop-ins?"

"No, I'm so sorry. The waiting list to join is over a year if you would like to be on the list," she told me.

"Ah, I understand. I used to train and play at a club with Sean years ago, and I just wanted my nephew to come by and at least see some good players. Would it be okay if we just watch for a little while?"

Sean was the younger player I used to practice with at the table tennis club in Northern Virginia years before. He may have lost a few games to me back then, but he was now the U.S. national champion and traveled around the world with top international teams.

"Oh, my gosh! You used to train with Sean?"

"Yes, we used to train together and play in tournaments when we were kids."

"You know," she whispered. "I would like to have you join and play tonight."

"That is so kind. Yes, we would like that very much. Thank you," I said, and she escorted us to an open table to warm up like VIPs.

After the lady in charge left us to our table, Dana said to me, clearly impressed with our good fortune, "This is some really good Ping-Pong karma."

"Yeah, I know. Pretty cool isn't it?"

The normal protocol was that you had to spot a group of players at about your skill level. Then you put your paddle down underneath the middle of their table to show them you were there to challenge the winner. We threw everything we had against some of the players, and won a few games here and there, so it was time well spent and we returned for several months.

A sanctioned tournament in Portland was coming up, and I talked Dana into heading down to see how well our sessions had prepared us. The highest-ranked players in the U.S. had ratings around 2600. We entered the bottom-feeder categories at the 1000 level. Sean, my training buddy from childhood and national champion, showed up to play in the open division. I spotted him sitting in the stands before his match and walked over to chat.

Sean told me that it still amazed him that simply hitting a little white ball over a net one more time than someone else had provided so many great things in life for him. I nodded, thinking to myself about some of the excellent times playing table tennis provided to me. We wished each other well as the announcers began directing players to the tables. Dana and I lost in the early rounds, but it was worth it to have Dana experience a tournament and to see Zach again. A few weeks later, Dad flew out from Florida and, with Dana in tow, we got into some excellent doubles matches with Jean's boyfriend, who played at a highly competitive table tennis club sponsored by his aerospace employer.

Dad remained active in tennis on the men's team that played against different clubs in Florida. Tennis was the central part of his life. For a couple of years, he had visited his mother's home country of Poland, and played in the annual tennis tournament in Krakow. He was the oldest and least skilled player to enter but always earned much appreciation from the locals for his effort.

Upon his return to the States, he repeated the Polish words *"Gin dobre"* several times a day with a big smile. I didn't know what it meant but I repeated it back to him when he said it, and we laughed as if there had never been any deep differences between us. But underneath the surface, I knew that I was never the son he would have wanted, and he was never father I would have hoped for. I think he knew it, too. He was a fighter. I was a lover. He was country. I was classic rock and roll. He was a hunter. I was a vegetarian. The list went on and on.

Good fortune smiled on my job prospects one morning when I saw a television infomercial. A gentleman was educating people about the benefits of juicing and hawking juice machines. I noticed the address for the company was in the area. Incredibly, a job posting appeared in the classifieds the next week. I applied and was soon part of the company. My holistic education was finally paying off. The fridge at the company headquarters was stocked with organic produce and we juiced ourselves up day after day until many of us turned orange from drinking so much carrot juice. I was in vegetarian heaven.

As if life couldn't get better, Scott, a barista across the street, and I struck up a table tennis conversation. The trash talking escalated and we soon set up a match. I played with smooth rubber that generated massive spins and he countered with his small pips that quickly blocked and neutralized my spins. The points were fast and furious, and each of us won a few games. Our friendship lead to an epic rivalry that continued amicably for years.

That year, Jean, Dana, and I flew out to Florida to visit Dad and play some tennis with him at his club. The grass courts there were expertly manicured, like the grass courts I had always wanted to play on at the Ambassador's house in Vientiane years ago. As much as I always dreamed of playing on a grass court, I was not prepared for the different bounce and timing that it produced and didn't enjoy it as much as I thought I would.

But these were the last days of playing with my old man, and I certainly didn't want to show any disappointment. Tennis had helped keep him active and youthful for many years but time was no longer on his side. He was slowing down and couldn't make the shots he used to make. Our days together as a formidable team were now over. It had been a long and memorable run, and I was sad that it was ending.

CHAPTER 12

Metaphysics with a Master Healer

On the way home, I pictured what Dad would be doing late that afternoon under the hot Florida sun. He'd be on his tiny concrete back porch with no shade listening to honky-tonk music through the screen door, while sipping Johnny Walker Red Label with some branch water on the rocks. He'd be laying on his cheap folding recliner asking himself, "What the hell happened?", kind of like Steve McQueen at the end of the movie *The Sand Pebbles*. My old man never believed in God. He said he was open to the idea there could actually be one, but he never pursued the matter any further.

But I still had enough motivation to keep up the search and wasn't giving up. Within a few weeks I spotted a poster for a psychic fair that was going to be held at a yoga center in the Lower Queen Anne neighborhood. I was interested in meeting a few intuitives to see if they had any special guidance on what I should do next. A good friend and tennis buddy from my college days, joined me that day. He was a skeptic but willing to indulge my curiosity. Inside the center, a couple of women wearing natural fiber clothing and hippie jewelry greeted us in the hallway.

One lady handed me a flier and explained, "The readings are 15 dollars and usually last around 15 minutes. You can do as many as you like."

That seemed like a reasonable amount for a minor adventure and so I signed up for three sessions and handed her 45 dollars. Looking at the written statements from each psychic about their sessions I then selected the ones who looked the most suitable.

The first psychic I sat down with was Dr. Vance. His eyes opened wide as he looked at me full of life and enthusiasm. Dr. Vance started off with a description on my chakras, from top to bottom with explanations on the colors he saw. He said I had past-life training as a monk in Tibet, and I thought that matched up well with my fascination with all things Tibetan.

He told me to open up my creativity in life and not be held back by fear. He said that I needed to face life like the Highlanders from Scotland on the mornings they faced battle: "IT'S A NICE DAY TO DIE!" he scribbled on his notepad in large capital letters to make sure I got the message. I thought it would be interesting to have a few beers with him sometime and hear more of his stories after he *really* loosened up.

The reader I chose next was an attractive lady about my age. She had wavy, brown hair that didn't quite reach her shoulders. Her name was Louise. She asked me to have a seat, and we began the session. Her method was to tell me a story while she created an artsy little card. She decorated it with shiny beads, sparkly buttons, and doodads from several plastic trays on her table. I was intrigued as she described my inner life and outer life with unusual accuracy. She described my search for deeper self-realization and that I had issues with my father that would need to be resolved. Each little item she glued onto the card had significance in the story she told, and represented part of the reading. I felt comforted by her insights and loveliness.

At the end of our time together she gave me the card so I would have a physical representation of the story she told. Curious about how she came up with such accurate information, I asked her about her ability.

"How does the information come to you?"

After reflecting for a moment, she answered, "The best way I can describe it is that I step out of my body during the session. Your soul then comes into my body and speaks with you through me. In this way, you get to have a conversation with a part of yourself you normally don't communicate with verbally or consciously. When the session is over, I return to my body and rarely recall anything that happened."

Wow! I was smitten. The other readers were interesting, but I was particularly moved by Louise's charm, so I continued to see Louise again at more of these fairs. Before long we were spending time together on our own, and we eventually became lovers as the natural attraction between us picked up steam. On some mornings, Louise woke up with physical effects left by the out-of-body work and travels she experienced during the sleep state. For example, if she had been typing in a library in another dimension while her physical body slept, the next morning her fingers would be physically tired or even sore. She also let me know in great detail when we taught courses together in the other dimension, but I was not conscious of teaching in these other-dimensional travels upon returning to the waking state.

Regarding her work as a psychic, Louise explained that she was able to obtain passage to the Akashic Records to help people attain information about their soul journeys. The Akashic Records are said to be a permanent recording of everything that happens or has ever happened, the vibratory imprint of every action and thought in the universe. "There is a gatekeeper," Louise explained. "To gain entrance you must produce the password... keeps the riff-raff out." She then laughed in her delightful way.

At the fairs where I met Louise there was another psychic I was interested in having a reading with, and so I did. She appeared to be in her 50s with short, curly hair and round glasses that looked a little large for her face; they gave her the appearance of a wise old owl. I sat down at her folding card table one afternoon to see what she had to say. She asked for my hands and held them gently as she closed her eyes.

After gathering information on intuitive levels, she opened her eyes slowly and said, "Ah, you are an experienced soul who lived during the days of Atlantis and helped out with the relocations before it was destroyed." Carol then mentioned a few other personal matters I was dealing with, and offered some guidance she felt would be helpful. Just before ending our chat, she added, "A man named Dennis Adams will be coming by the area in a few weeks. I think you would enjoy seeing him. He teaches metaphysical workshops, and is about at the avatar level."

When people in metaphysics use the word "avatar," they are often referring to the Sanskrit meaning, which when loosely translated means "someone who is self-realized and operates from that level of awareness."

I, of course, was very interested in finding out if there was anyone out there like that, so I attended the free-preview lecture in one of the buildings on the Seattle waterfront. The year was 1990 and at 29 years of age I was beginning to feel a little worried that my search for self-realization and enlightenment was not producing results.

Once I got settled into my seat along with the other attendees, Dennis walked in with a big smile. He was tall and lanky, and had a swarthy look befitting his Italian ancestry. Sporting a long ponytail and beard, he paced back and forth and told us a few humorous stories about the human condition. After hearing his brief talk, and seeing him laugh at his own jokes, I was not so impressed that I wanted to spend 300 dollars I didn't have to attend his two-day workshop, but I signed up anyway and put it on my credit card. I had come this far in my search and didn't have much to show for it, so I rationalized, *Why not go a little further just in case enlightenment was around the next corner?* I had come too far to give up just yet. Little did I know at the time that I was just beginning to open the door which would lead me into the world of mysteries and experiences that would transform my life in many ways.

On the morning of the first day of the workshop, there were about 100 of us sitting in rows of chairs in a large banquet hall. Dennis walked in and introduced himself saying, "Well, hello there. My name is Dennis Adams. I'm not an ET. I'm not a walk-in. I'm not a channel. And I'm not an ET, walk-in, channel. I'm just a normal guy from Cleveland. And anything I can do, so can you."

He asked for a show of hands. "How many people are in pain?" About four people raised their hands. Then he said, "Let's try this again. How many of you are in some form of physical, mental, emotional, or spiritual pain?" Just about everyone lifted a hand in the air and he laughed and said, "Whew! I thought I was in the wrong room like this was a real estate convention or something."

Everyone laughed when he broke the ice with that one. Then he had each of us walk up to the front and state what we wanted to get out of the workshop. Some asked for help with specific health or personal problems. One person asked for clarity. A young guy in his 20s with spiked, bleached hair asked for a white Lamborghini; it never showed up. I asked to learn about giving and receiving unconditional love.

We showed up the next morning in various types of pajamas, sweatpants, and blue jeans. A few curled up on sleeping bags, blankets, and pillows like it was a sleepover. I had absolutely no clue what we were going to do, but I thought my experiences at the Himalayan ashram would get me through whatever might come up. As long as we wouldn't have to do any role-playing...I hated role-playing. So I hunkered down, listened, and took notes while Dennis spoke. Oddly enough, he gave us permission to sleep through his workshop if we felt like it, telling us that he would still get the material through to our various bodies and subconscious minds. He added that the personality can create barriers of resistance to new information, especially if it was coming from someone else's mouth, and one can more easily assimilate and absorb the material while asleep.

To brief us on his background, he spoke about being born with the ability to access knowledge from his previous lives. As a child, the incredible pain from multiple surgeries drove him to learn how to project his consciousness outside of his body, as a technique to get away from the pain from which none of the painkilling drugs provided relief. As a result, he was able to leave his body on command, control it from a remote distance, and stay conscious when he traveled outside of it.

When he was in his 20s, Dennis had been active in metaphysical groups and became president of the Annie Besant lodge of the Theosophical Society in Cleveland. Raised as a Catholic, his spiritual path had also led him to become a priest in the Liberal Catholic Church, in which the famous clairvoyant, C.W. Leadbeater, once held a leadership position. Having a strong affinity and appreciation for Theosophical wisdom, I was excited that I had this in common with Dennis.

Dennis left Cleveland and the priesthood to spend the next eight years living alone in the Sierra Mountains in California, naked and surrounded by nature, to learn what he could on his own. Actually, he wasn't alone all of the time—Dennis said there were occasions when the same beings who worked with Madame Blavatsky in the 1800s, materialized and trained him in order to expand his knowledge and paranormal capabilities. This really got my attention.

He then said that one day, out of nowhere, the universe informed him that he was now a healer and that it was time to leave the woods and share the knowledge that was given to him. He was initially resistant but could feel that the universe was serious on this one and was eventually going to push him out of the forest one way or the other. So he reluctantly made his way out of the wilderness and renewed his contact with society.

In California he crossed paths with a renowned astrophysicist, and other researchers such as Stan Krippner. They studied his paranormal abilities under laboratory conditions, along with other well-known remote viewers and healers like Olga Worrall and proved that among other things, the power of the mind could alter the physical world of matter.

During the rest of the workshop, Dennis went into fascinating detail about topics of great interest to me and he also had many practical and simple tips for all of us. He described humans as having several bodies—the feeling body, the physical body, the emotional body, the mental body, and the spiritual aspect as well. The chakras buttoned all of them together and pulled in and stepped down the electromagnetic energy, known as *prana* in Sanskrit, from the sun. The heart chakra is where the descending energy from spirit mixes with the ascending energy of evolution as pictured in the geometric form known as the Star of David. "The top three chakras belong to God, and the bottom three belong to Man," he told us. "When descending spiritual energy and the ascending evolutionary energy merge in the heart, represented by the symbol of the Star of David, you become a God-man."

His description of the various interpenetrating bodies sounded like the *koshas* in Sanskrit literature, so a lot of what he was saying made sense to me. Dennis said that each human was a microcosm of the macrocosm and everyone could experience this as being an individual within the One-ness of totality. He also described how consciousness used the world of matter to express and evolve itself, through the mineral, vegetable, animal, and then into the human kingdoms. By now I was on the edge of my seat listening to his mesmerizing stories.

Dennis continued, "Let's talk about the moment you show up as a fetus. Medical scientists have footage of this and it's so cool. You have to see it. During the first few frames, there is nothing but thousands of little points of light, and then in the blink of an eye, the dots of light instantly merge and then—*shazam!*—a fetus appears. So don't worry. Every cell in your body remembers that you came from light. You'll be able to turn into light when you need to. Don't make a run at it just yet though," he advised.

"During the first seven years on earth, your cellular growth rate is at a seven-to-one ratio compared to an adult," he said. "This means everything that happens to you during those years takes on a huge seven-to-one significance compared to the rest of your life. During those early years you take on the patterns of your parents at a massive seven-to-one ratio. Like it or not, you become like your parents and their personalities express through you several times an hour. You love your parents so unconditionally that you even take on the same diseases and health problems they have. At an early age you saw how long your grandparents or relatives were living and formulated how long you thought you would live. You are already planning your death by creating a picture of when you think it should happen."

Dennis suggested that if we want to begin to change our lives, that we "do something different early in the morning that breaks your usual routine. Flush the toilet with your left hand instead of your right hand, or whatever. Just change even one thing you normally do early in the day and it will change your whole day. You need to break out of the rut you are stuck in."

He also warned us not to sleep near any containers with open alcohol, as disembodied spirits from the astral plane are attracted to the vapors because it makes them feel almost alive again. We were advised to sleep with our heads pointing north to be in better magnetic flow with the way energy moves on the planet, and to firmly shake or replace the pillows on our beds more frequently. If we were trying to change our concepts and grow, we should not put our heads down every night into the same old thoughts and worries for eight hours.

This was exactly the type of information I had sought my entire life, so I took notes furiously to keep track of all the suggestions that were being provided. Some people remained alert and a few drifted off to sleep. They missed some really good stuff even if they got the spiritual material as they slept. Dennis had a bawdy, wonderful sense of humor that came from his rough and tumble Cleveland upbringing. He apologized for his strong language, but those who stayed awake laughed with him at his stories and antics because they came from the heart and he couldn't help being himself.

One of his trademark stories was about his search to find out if God really exists. He called it "The Space Story." It seemed most of the people had heard it before, but no one could stop him from telling it. The story goes like this: After several years of living in the woods to gain wisdom away from society, Dennis decided that if this thing called God really exists, he should be able to prove it to himself beyond a shadow of a doubt. Then he sat down and gave himself two weeks because he felt that it shouldn't take any longer than that if he was really looking hard. (I won't be able to do justice to his telling of the rest of this story, but you can hear him speak about it on the Internet.) The important thing to remember is that the deeper into matter you look, if you go down to the atomic level, the amount of space increases so much that, mathematically speaking, the world of matter is made up of empty space more than anything else. And space, as you know, contains a massive amount of energy. When you smash space together, you get what's called "nuclear fusion." All God had to do was hug itself to create the Big Bang and the rest of creation as we know it. Space is eternal, omnipresent, and everything and everyone is connected through it. It made sense to Dennis that space meets the criteria for being God. Made sense to me, too.

After a lunch break, it came time to teach us how to project ourselves out of our bodies, and Dennis taught us what he called "The Stand Up, Sit Down" technique, and how to use angels to fill us up with whatever we felt we needed, whether it was vitamin B-12, unconditional love, or anything, really. It was like some form of particle-wave homeopathy using the feeling body. And it was so simple it only took us about 10 minutes to learn, practice, and experience results. I was feeling results right away and was amazed to see how easy most of his techniques were. They worked whether or not you believed they would and they worked whether or not you were doing them right. This was good stuff and I knew I was finally hot on the spiritual trail! Then he taught us how to take our bodies back in time and release karma that was still trapped within us. Some people experienced massive transformations as we all walked in a circle, following Dennis' instructions as he spoke.

Dennis said that he found through observations and multi-dimensional travels that electrons carry information from our physical units into the invisible world of space, which surrounds every particle of matter. We update the rest of the universe through the space with our own electrons, and they come back into our body with unconditional love, along with updates on what everything else in existence is up to. By increasing the amount of unconditional love within the electrons in the body, you increase the energy in them to the point where the electron doubles and then triples itself to handle the increase of energy. At this point the physical body simply disappears from sight because it has accelerated into a higher rate of frequency than the human eyes can see.

If God is space and space exists within everything, then as the electrons go back and forth between our bodies and the space that connects all that exists, we are basically playing tennis with God all the time with our electrons…even (and especially) when we are sleeping. To my delightful surprise, I was learning that life is basically a cosmic tennis rally with the rest of the universe. We get to choose our own shots in life, see how they work out, and how we feel about them. When we hit a good shot in tennis or in life, we know it because of how it makes us feel. When we hit a bad shot, we know that, too, because it just doesn't feel right or it doesn't achieve the result we desired. Whatever our game in sports or in life, to improve it, all we have to do is pay attention to what we are doing in the present moment and observe what kind of feedback the universe gives us. Then we can make the adjustments that feel better and hopefully achieve the outcomes and improvements we seek.

I was blown away by all of the new information from Dennis and it sat well with me. At the end of the second and final day, Dennis summarized a few points and then wrapped it up by saying to us, "Blessings on you and all that you see." Everyone picked up their blankets and pillows and gave hugs to their friends. I waited a few moments to ask him a question before I left. He noticed me standing near him and took a few steps over to me. Before I could ask the question I had in mind, Dennis bent down and kissed me on the top of my head. It struck me as a strange greeting since we had only just met.

"What information from this weekend can I share with others?" I asked him.

"Everything except for the "Stand Up, Sit Down" technique. If you teach that to someone and you can't get them back into their body, you are still responsible for the karma."

I nodded in acknowledgement, and then he gave me a goodbye hug. *I'll have to get used to hugs if I want to hang out with this crowd,* I thought.

Dennis came through town to teach four times each year and I attended each weekend no matter how much I had to keep adding onto my credit cards. In addition to that, each month he recorded cassette tapes near the top of Mount Shasta and sent them out to anyone who wanted to be in what he called the "Fellowship Group." After a year of being in the "Support Group," I joined his Fellowship Group as well, which allowed me to hear the monthly tapes that were quite humorous and packed with paranormal events and enlightened information. I could also take workshops in other cities for a reduced fee. Dennis was always surrounded by people who wanted his time and attention, and although I stayed on the periphery I watched every move he made.

As much as I disliked doing affirmations, Dennis taught us his versions and I began to practice them. I was willing to do almost anything he recommended, because the healing miracles and results he was producing were quite impressive. I wanted to be in on the action, big time. I practiced saying affirmations on the inhalations and exhalations, so that our inner and outer space and consciousness would be strengthened by the positive messages. One of his favorites was, "I love you, God." We repeated it several times on the inhale, holding our breaths and the blessings inside of ourselves for as long as it took to inhale, then repeated it on the exhale. Another was, "I am in the right place, and this is the right time."

"If you use that affirmation," he told us, "when the universe is looking for someone who is at the right place at the right time, you'll at least have a shot at whatever it is going to pop out."

The professional tennis world had also seen the result of Dennis' healing abilities. He had done healing work on the knee of a professional tennis player who had a significant injury. After some treatment with Dennis, the player won a championship at Wimbledon. *This is too cool,* I thought to myself. *Tennis and metaphysics are interweaving right in front of me.* This was an obvious sign that as weird as things were getting, somehow I was on the right track.

I continued practicing many of the techniques Dennis provided, and did the "stripping technique" on my legs in the shower every day to remove any thought forms I wanted to let go of. Another one of Dennis' techniques was a hot/cold treatment at the nearby Stewart Mineral Springs resort. You do a mineral bath soak and then go into the wood-fired sauna to get heated to the core, and then some. Then you go for a dip in the cold creek outside, staying in the water long enough to cool down the body as much as you can stand, and then some beyond that. The process is repeated three times for the full effect of undergoing the changes in consciousness that come with the heating and cooling cycles. He told us that this technique would show us through observation that the frequencies of hot and cold don't come from this dimension. I tried it several times and became seriously altered—but even if the frequency of coldness comes from another dimension, it was still too damn cold in this one!

Another of the techniques used at some of the workshops was the "hugging exercise." In preparation for that one Dennis said to us, "Everyone pick out a partner, someone you are going to feel comfortable hugging for a long time. And you are not allowed to choose the person you came with. Pick someone you don't know."

Oh great, I thought. Hugging was one of my weak points. There were a few awkward moments while we made cautious eye contact with strangers and matched up.

After we paired up, he went on with the instructions, "When you do your hugs, I want you to have all of your chakras lined up with your partner—don't pooch your butts out! Hugs with pooches are not real hugs and I'm going to call you on it if I see it. After a few minutes you'll notice that energy will rise up from the lower chakras. Ladies, if you are hugging a male partner, you may notice him become awake in the lower chakra area. Do not be embarrassed and don't freak out. The energy will eventually move upward and open the higher chakras; so just stay in the hug and don't take it personally. When you get into the hug, I want you to stay in it until I say we are done. Okay, everybody get with your partner and begin."

At this point there were a hundred of us in pairs, hugging each other very closely. After a few minutes, the room started to get warmer; and as we settled into the hugs, the room became silent except for some breathing and bodies shifting position. It wasn't long before I noticed the breathing pattern between my partner and I had established so that when my stomach was expanding on the inhale, hers was retracting. A gentle, natural rhythm was established that worked for both bodies. Dennis asked us to hold the person closely and give them as much love as we would give to a small baby, or to our inner child, and then even to God. The room became even warmer and, as we stayed in our hugs, I entered a state where it felt like I was not even holding anyone. And no one was holding me. I just existed in a state of pure unconditional love and it felt great.

Then Dennis said to us quietly, "Okay, you can come out of your hugs now and open your eyes slowly as you come back into your body." He then chuckled, "Heh, heh, heh." We came out of our hugs and, as everyone separated, smiles grew on our faces and there was silence for quite a few minutes because the hugs had taken us into a deeply blissful state. I had never been a real hugger before but I could see this technique might become one of my all-time favorites. I showed my girlfriend Louise how it worked and she loved it as well.

Money is a concern for most people and Dennis began working on our money issues along with other matters we struggled with. He was trying to raise the value we had for ourselves. One month we received a tape from Dennis saying that he could really use our help financially. He said that if we each sent him 24 dollars, he would be covered. I was still paying off student loans from living in the ashram graduate school, but scraped together the 24 dollars and sent him a check.

The next month he sent another tape that thanked everyone who either sent or didn't send the money. He had no judgments and told us that he always wanted us to be true to ourselves. Then Dennis reported that about one-third of his students were so offended by him asking for 24 dollars, that they were not going to study with him any longer. About six months later he asked the remaining students for an additional 50 dollars to help him out, and he lost another big chunk of the group. Now we were down to about a hundred or so of the group members. But each time the ante upped, I was in. All in. The depth of knowledge we were receiving and paranormal events we were participating in were too big of an attraction for me.

The people who wanted or needed his help or attention always surrounded Dennis. To spend personal time with him, I saved up enough money to have a private healing appointment. I set that up and then met him in his hotel room. He let me in the room, and we chatted for a bit.

"What have you got going on that we need to handle?" he asked.

"Nothing that I can think of. Maybe just a small tune-up," I stated.

"Oh. Okay. Well, let's have you take your belt and any other metal off. Get up onto the table and lay down on your back."

There was a massage table in the room. I took my shoes off and climbed onto the table.

Dennis stood down at my feet and said, "Lift your left leg and see how heavy it is."

I raised my left foot. Then we repeated the same for my other leg.

"Which one is heavier?" he asked.

"The right one."

"Okay. I'm going to slide my hands down the right leg."

He had shown us the "stripping" concept in the workshops and I had been stripping my legs every day in the shower.

The sun is a positive charge, he had told us, and the Earth is a negative ground. Energy enters the human body at the place where the hair spirals near the back of the head and runs down the *nadis*, the electromagnetic pathways of the body. (These are the lines you see on the acupuncture charts that look like little train tracks.)

Placing his hands around my thigh, he slid them slowly down my leg and pulled the energy off my feet. Then he tossed it at a lit candle that was on the desk.

He repeated this two more times then asked me to lift my leg to see if there was any difference.

"Yep, it's lighter," I told him.

Then he did the same technique on my left leg, and proceeded to do the same on the rest of my body. For some reason, although he was barely touching me, he seemed to be exerting a strong effort and he began sweating even though the room felt almost chilly to me.

Then he spun his index finger in the air above my solar plexus.

"Just speeding up your chakra a little," he chuckled.

At the end of the session he placed his hands on my heart, relaxed them, and stayed silent for a few minutes. He explained that since he had just stripped out a lot of old thought forms that were no longer serving me, he was now filling me back up with unconditional love. This would fill the space so that I would not feel empty and so that material from other people, places, and things would not flood back in.

"How do you feel?" he asked.

"I feel good." At that moment I didn't have a care in the world and felt very much at peace.

"This is your natural state. You should feel like that all the time," he said with a big grin.

"Thanks so much," I told him as his next appointment knocked on the door. "I'll see you this weekend."

"All right, my brother. Take care."

We hugged and I went out the door.

***

At the next workshop Dennis told us emphatically, "You folks are always telling me how much you think about God. The truth is, you don't think about God much at all. So, this is what I want you to do to see for yourself: Just try to think about God for three minutes during each hour you are awake. Just three minutes. And let me know how it goes when I see you again in a few months."

Most of us went out and tried that. But it annoyed so many of us that we were not capable of even thinking of God for three minutes an hour that a dozen people gave up and quit attending the workshops. I saw how hard it was to maintain such a focus, but I persevered and didn't quit trying.

Each month Dennis sent us a tape to inspire and teach us. For four years Dennis recorded an audio series for the Fellowship high atop Mount Shasta, calling it *Stepping Into the Consciousness*. He only went up the mountain and recorded a talk when he perceived the universe had something special to share. After several hours of deep meditation at an altitude of 9,000 feet—to which he said no human thought forms were able to rise—Dennis shared his insights and experiences in his entertaining and humorous style. I immersed myself in the tapes and applied their lessons to my life the best I could. He had a few basic teachings that he reminded us of over and over again: lighten up; don't take things personally; it's never outside of yourself; don't judge anything; what you give your truth to becomes your reality; and, stay in the present moment.

During certain workshops, we went just where I wanted to go: further and further into the metaphysical world. In some of the guided meditations, we had out-of-body experiences. Dennis guided us into an unseen dimension where there was a golden pyramid in a desert. We entered and sat in a particle-accelerator chair like the one mentioned in Guy Ballard's books that produced the "I Am" spiritual movement in America in the 1930s. At times we drank elixirs mixed by masters to assist our progress. We mixed a few elixirs ourselves when, on rare occasions, Dennis broke out his priest kit and performed a brief ritual with water and wine. Alcohol absorbs blessings placed upon it and the vapors carry the blessings deep into the body. There were also quite a few times at our yearly gatherings when interesting miracles occurred. One day at a workshop near Seattle, miracles happened to be the main topic. Dennis opened a blue velvet pouch and brought out a rosary while he told us its story: A woman had brought it to Medjugorje, Yugoslavia, and had gone to the hill where the Mother Mary apparitions appeared, to ask for healing for her father who was dying of cancer.

The apparition appeared to her with the message her father would be healed, but she still wanted a sign to validate that the message was real. On the trip home from Europe, she noticed that the silver connections between the wooden beads on the rosary had turned to gold. She saw this as the sign she was hoping for and, when she returned to the States, she learned that her father was cured.

Now the rosary had been given to Dennis. He let each of us hold it during the workshop as he taught. A woman who had been holding onto the rosary for a long time went into the bathroom during a break. When she looked in the mirror, she noticed something was going on with her silver filigree necklace. She came out of the bathroom and stood next to Dennis and me, and let him hold it up for us to observe. We then watched the rest of the necklace change slowly from silver to gold. The transition started at one end and moved along until the entire piece was completely gold. "Miracles," Dennis explained, "are a state of consciousness that can override the laws of physics. If you acknowledge them when you see them, they are more likely to show up and participate in your reality."

That workshop was the only one I attended where children were allowed to be present. At one point Dennis sat down with them in a circle at the front of the room, just two feet in front of me (I was in the front row with an unobstructed view). They joined hands at his request, then he had them look at the color of one of their shirts and said, "Everyone look at the color of that shirt. Let's create that color right in front of us in the middle of the circle." The kids and Dennis focused for a few moments. Then, on the ground in the middle of the circle a small flame appeared that was the color of the child's shirt they were trying to replicate. He picked another color from one of their shirts and they did it again. I watched in amazement each time a new color appeared out of thin air. And they did it again, for three times in a row.

Speaking of things that come out of thin air, my relationship with Louise took a sharp turn one evening.

"Brian, if we are not going to get married, then we need to stop seeing each other," she told me with conviction. "I don't want to get hurt."

I checked in with my inner feelings and told her, "I'm not ready for marriage right now, Louise, but I understand where you are coming from."

"I'm going to miss you," she said with tears streaming down her face.

"I'm going to miss you, too," I said as we hugged goodbye.

Our brief yet deep cosmic relationship ended with both of us in tears and nothing left to say. *How many times will my heart have to be broken?* I wondered to myself as I drove home in the rain.

By this time the unusual had now become usual to me; the paranormal had become normal, as it were. One person I met at Dennis' workshops, Keith, told me of his experience meeting the Rinpoche from a Buddhist temple near Mount Shasta who placed an energy diamond into his heart as a gift. Keith swears the guy was one of the Four Lords of the Flame. There was also a story about the Buddha visiting Mount Shasta. Apparently there was an elderly woman named Sister Thedra who lived in the city of Mount Shasta. The Buddha used to manifest inside her house for visits. And there was also Pearl, a woman who was written about in the "I Am" spiritual books that Guy Ballard wrote. She lived in the Mount Shasta area before she made her final transition. The ascended master Saint Germain was said to materialize and work with her.

At the end of one particular workshop things began to become almost biblical. Dennis anointed our feet with a fragrant oil from Egypt in the most humble way you could imagine. The oil was made from special flowers handpicked by clairvoyants who were able to see which ones carried the strongest energy. He made the sign of the cross with his thumb between our eyes and said, "In the name of the one true God." Later he explained that the Illuminati had kept the bloodline of Jesus going so that when the Christ Consciousness returned to the Earth, it would possess a few of the physical units that could handle more of it, and thus control the destiny of the planet. He said, "The problem with their plan, though, is that when you overbreed a good stock, it can become too high strung and mentally unstable. Only the mutts will be able to handle this kind of energy. Be glad you're a mutt."

Attending a psychic and health fair, 1990

Dennis Adams

There are times in history when individuals feel the spark of the divine plan within and become the archetypal inspiration for others. Dennis Adams is one of these special beings. He is "one of the most powerful psychics with whom I have worked." *quote-Elizabeth Rauscher, Ph.D.- Renowned Physicist.* Dennis is different. He is able to affect substance and matter of human cells by consciously altering perception of time and space, proving that life essence is mutable and can be changed by the power of the mind. He lives in Mt. Shasta and through a discipline lasting twenty two years has uncovered the secrets that make him "the finest healer the world now knows." *quote-Olga Worrall, Ph.D.-PSI Researcher*

Conciousness
The Final Frontier
FREE PREVIEWS
❏ Tues., Nov. 3- 7:30PM
  Airport Hilton, Theater Room
  5711 W. Century Blvd., L.A.
❏ Wed., Nov. 4- 7:30PM
  The Registry Hotel, Salon 6A
  555 Universal Terrace Pkwy.,
  (above Sheraton Universal)
L.A. Workshop Information
❏ November 6, 7, & 8
  ($350 if pre-registered with
  $50 deposit by Nov. 5)

Dennis
Adams
Seminars

P.O. Box 1319
Mt. Shasta, CA 96067
916/925-3196

For registration or information
contact

Advertisement for a Dennis Adams Seminars
metaphysical and personal growth workshop

On grass courts with Dad, Jean, and nephew
Dana at Dad's tennis club in Florida

My father during a jovial moment before Parkinson's disease set in

CHAPTER 13

Tennis with God

Fifteen years ago I had promised Paul, my high school buddy from Bogota, we would keep in touch. It took a while but I tracked him down in Southern California where he had been living with his wife and young daughter. In Los Angeles, we lined up a reunion match at a hotel on Sunset Boulevard.

At the time I was playing tennis every week and had worked my way up to the number-one court during men's doubles' night at the club I played at. It had taken weeks of constantly proving myself by winning month after month to move up in the ranks. These were the same courts where I had watched the old Australian pros play and met Rod Laver in the parking lot years earlier. But now I had reached my own level of tennis nirvana. Every time I played, my shots were at such a high level and the touches and angles were so dialed in, I could hardly believe it. All I had to do was swing my racket and the balls sailed in with laser-guided precision. My first serve had incredible pop and velocity, my backhand had finally shaped up, and I was playing better than I ever thought possible. I was in my own little Roger sublime Federer zone every time I stepped onto the court.

The night before Paul and I played, we raided the mini-bar in the hotel room like we were still in high school, and played some faux points in the room as well, bouncing balls off the walls, doors, and pictures. The next morning, slightly hungover, we walked to the court along a row of tall palm trees to the court beside the hotel. During the warm-up, I admired Paul's polished strokes. His crisp, flat backhands skidded when they hit the court and came at me faster than I expected. It was so great just to be hitting back and forth with one of my best friends. But this could also be the best chance I would have to catch him by surprise and score an upset win. No, make that a *huge* upset win.

The match began and I held serve, getting mine in with enough power to let him know I was to be reckoned with. By the third game I had him 3-0. Paul was still settling into his game, so if I was going to win I had to keep up my level of play faster than he could gear up. He came back and won the next two games and then we moved to 5-4 in my favor. I paused for a moment. I noticed that I was winning but not having the sense of joy I wanted to have. I was too focused on winning.

So, I relaxed my attitude and allowed myself to just fully enjoy such a rare occasion of playing with Paul instead of trying to be ruthless and get a win at all costs. I even gave him all the close line calls just to make sure I wasn't attached to winning. It was a loss I enjoyed more than many of my big wins.

At the end of the set, Paul made some solid shots and won, just before one of the hotel clerks came out to inform us that our time was up.

"If we had time for another set, I think I might have had you," I told him jokingly. I was pleased that I had stayed true to the reason I loved playing: just for the pure joy of the game.

Things were going well for me, or so I thought. My tennis game was at the highest level ever, and I was studying with the world's best metaphysical teacher, and learning the secrets of the universe. I had also recently married Setsuko, a woman from Japan that I had been seeing. We struck a good balance in many ways. She even attended a few workshops with Dennis and then left me to them as she needed to spend time on her own interests, hiking and kayaking. Being in nature was her way of experiencing God and creation, she told me.

***

I was in Mount Shasta one weekend and Dennis turned to me as we were driving to lunch and said, "Life doesn't work like you think it does." He continued in a direct, almost challenging manner, "You glance off things and don't take them head on. If you really want to be a spiritual warrior, you are going to have to change your approach."

He was calling me out on my strategy of avoidance and I knew he was right. I had avoided confrontation with my father all those years and I didn't know how to stand up for myself. Dennis was all about taking things head on and breaking any patterns that limited him. He said that quitting my job and coming to Mount Shasta to give him a hand would also help "break my attachment to the physical plane."

Break my attachment to the physical plane? I wasn't sure what that looked like so I was a little apprehensive. I wasn't really sure I was ready to live on the spiritual razor's edge that Dennis was used to. But the opportunity was before me and I had to make a choice.

There is a moment in the *Bhagavad Gita* when Arjuna faces a momentous decision: He was faced with going into battle against a group of his own relatives. He had to pick either a huge army with the most effective weapons and resources, or head into the fray with only a tiny blue chap named Krishna as his charioteer. But Krishna is an incarnation of God, so Arjuna chooses him; and so, of course, they win the battle. You can't lose if God is in your corner.

It was now time for me to choose sides. Was I going to stay hitched to the world of matter or step into the ephemeral world of spirit and trust that things would work out? Was I going to quit my new job and risk damaging my new marriage to follow a radical spiritual teacher who challenged the rules of physics and society, and expected everyone around him to raise their game to his level? This kind of opportunity might never be offered to me again and so I considered it very carefully.

"All right," I informed Dennis. "I would like to come to Mount Shasta. When should I come?"

"I need you in May," he replied.

May was only two months away, earlier than I had expected, but I went ahead and planned for my deployment. My length of stay was unknown and indefinite. I gave Setsuko the unexpected news and was not surprised that she was not as excited as I was about my move to Mount Shasta. However, I told her that it was necessary for me to go

(I truly felt it was), and so she made the adjustment as lovingly as she could under the circumstances. Descending the steep curves through the mountains of Southern Oregon and then the Siskiyou Pass, I caught a glimpse of snow atop Mount Shasta and wondered what the mountain might have in store for me. I pulled up in front of Dennis and Jessica's house, and got out of my rig hoping that I was ready for anything. Dennis walked out of the open garage and said, "Hey, Mr. Wimbledon. Welcome home." He knew I liked to play tennis at the courts in town with the locals when I visited in the past. One of his students, Greg, and I had also developed quite a rivalry.

"Your tan is looking good for this early in the year," I complimented him.

He pointed to his face, "See the deep purple color? That's not from the sun. The sun hasn't really been out for two weeks. I'm cooking the meat from the inside."

My mind flashed back to a day where I remember him giving a demonstration to a few of us. He stood up, went silent, and began increasing the frequency of his body until it was generating a wave of heat that spread for 30 feet in each direction. People sitting in the first row were starting to sweat. I was sitting farthest away by an open window and felt the heat wave reach me. He stopped the process and returned to normal consciousness and said, "Now that your consciousness has recorded how to do this, you'll be able to pull it off in the future if you need to. Any questions?"

The group was so stunned that nobody had any questions, even the ones that always asked lots of them.

Then Dennis brought me back into the present moment when he said, "Hey, the bees up in the garden are getting ready to swarm. Come on."

He grabbed some work gloves from his garage and as we walked briskly he asked, "Did you know that bees were brought from Venus to give mankind a model for working together as a community under a female leader?"

I answered, "Never heard that one." He was always sharing side stories you would never hear anywhere else.

We hurried up to the area where the bees had swarmed out of their hives into a nearby tree. Then in seconds they lifted off in a thick buzzing mass and floated off into the woods.

"Looks like they're gone. I don't think they're coming back," he said with disappointment in his voice.

"I have to head into town and find a place to stay," I told him as we walked back to the house.

"There's a room for rent in the house behind the health-food store in town…the one made of stone right off Main Street. Go check it out and let's have dinner tonight about eight when Jess gets home."

"Okay, I'll see you then."

At the health-food store in the city of Weed I met the deli clerk who had the room for rent. I accepted the deal and moved right in. In a few days I knew I was really on the fringes of society when my new housemate told me that he was on the run from people in the government who were messing with him over his experiments with plasma and free energy. "They are looking to kill me," he told me with a serious look when he was practicing moves with his Samurai sword one morning. He showed me some photos of the work he was doing and it looked like something Nicola Tesla would be interested in.

Starting with the very first day, I learned that hanging out with Dennis meant trying to stay in the present moment like he did, which was difficult for me at times. I liked the past. The past had been pretty good to me. To help me stay in present moment, Dennis mentioned a novel approach that I had never heard before. He said that instead of going back into the past, I should just bring the past into the present, especially the wonderful moments in life where I had felt very connected or aware.

"Even though a special moment may have passed by quickly, you recorded it with your consciousness," he told me. "That knowingness is still with you, so bring it to you in the present when you need it. Don't stay in the past. Pay attention to what you are doing in the present moment," he said. "Whatever you are creating for yourself in the present moment is most likely what you will be creating in a future present moment. If you are creating unhappiness right now, you will most likely be creating unhappiness in a future present moment."

Life became especially interesting when Dennis and Jessica, who was his business manager and now was also his wife, held events like their annual Healing Week. For that one, a large hall was rented, and people who wanted to learn natural healing techniques came from all over the country with their massage tables. Jess was becoming a fine healer in her own right, and working closely with Dennis on a daily basis had further improved her abilities. This was an incredible opportunity for me to learn from both of them, and to begin to learn the healing arts and support their work.

During the first two days we learned some of the basic understandings of the methods and techniques. The "stripping technique" was the primary healing method we were taught. It was effective in clearing the electromagnetic pathways in the body, and pulling out the thought forms and pain from the body that a person was ready to release. Then hands were placed on the client's body where they felt they needed to be healed, and unconditional love flowed in to replace whatever the client had released.

Dennis asked for a volunteer from among the participants. Using the person who stood up, he stood beside the man and asked us, "Does anyone see what is going on with him?"

We looked the man up and down, but nobody noticed anything obvious. Then Dennis pointed to the man's right shoulder area. "See how this one side slumps just slightly, and is jammed just a bit right here? It is not as open as the other side."

Once he had pointed it out, it became easier to spot. He explained further, "During birth, his body became stressed on this side, and is still holding onto the trauma. Many people still have these types of issues because being born is a very difficult process." Dennis had spent time in the late 1970s studying with people who had developed the rebirthing technique as a therapeutic treatment. He asked the gentleman to get onto the massage table and had him lie down.

Starting at the top of the man's head, Dennis put his arms around him. Then he slid his arms down the length of the man's body to give him the experience of a new birth without any trauma. After Dennis pulled his arms all the way off the man's feet, he asked the man to stand. The gentleman stood up, and when he did, it was clear that the trauma had been released. He was more upright and balanced, his posture was more open, and the right side of his body didn't slump as it had before.

Watching this happen so effortlessly I thought to myself, *This is going to be so easy. I'll be a world-class healer in no time.* That fantasy lasted less than two hours when I found out that I would be expected to work on real clients during the last two days of the workshop. During the last few days, the public showed up for free, one-hour appointments. Mild panic set in as the reality confronted me that I was still just a tennis player in holistic clothing. I didn't know a thing about creating healing miracles on demand but it was too late to back out.

A few dozen clients had made appointments, traveled from all over to be there, and were lined up outside the main door. Many had serious health issues, and they expected miraculous results. There were about 12 bodywork tables, with one or two healers at each table. I was by myself at one table. All the other healers looked like they knew what they were doing, and this increased my feelings of inadequacy. Some had backgrounds in Reiki, massage, and other modalities.

A local musician was sent over to my table for a healing. He walked over and I introduced myself. Then I asked him to describe what parts of his body were having problems or didn't feel good. After he told me what was going on, I circled the problem areas on a chart that had a drawing of a body. Then I had him get onto the massage table, and I began to use the energy-stripping technique I had learned. I made him lift each leg and tell me which one was heavier. Then I started on that leg. I did the technique on each of his legs three times to see if he noticed a difference.

"Yeah. It feels lighter."

"Great. You're letting go of thoughts that don't serve you," I replied with a line similar to ones that Dennis used.

After that kind of confirmation, you know the client is aware of the change. Then you proceed to the other leg, the arms, upper body, and head. I was not used to putting my hands on anyone's body in this manner, especially another man, so it felt awkward.

Meanwhile, Dennis wandered around the hall, giving people assistance and encouragement here or there, and "keeping the angels from jumping in to help," as he had told us. Angels apparently like to lend a hand at the slightest encouragement, but this was our time to learn as much as we could on our own. Being thoroughly nervous I moved through my healing motions on the musician rather quickly. I was used to the lightning-quick speed of table tennis. But healing was about slowing down and being intuitive so I was coming from the wrong perspective. All of my prior training in sports was working against me. In about 10 minutes I told him we were done and thought that was it. But it wasn't really over. Dennis was standing behind me and had seen my performance. He said sternly, "You need to finish working on him. You haven't even started."

Damn! He was right. I didn't know what in the hell I was doing. So I got back to work with the energy-stripping technique with even more focus. I slowed down and took more time. After 20 more minutes of that, I had the gentleman sit up and put his shoes back on. He thanked me for the session. I bought one of the musician's CDs and felt mostly embarrassed at how little I really knew about doing this type of work. Jessica saw that I didn't have another client waiting and said, "We need you over here."

I walked over to Jessica's table, and there was a boy about nine years old laying on it who had a heart condition that left him barely able to stay in his body. His father had carried him inside. The boy's skin was very pale, his eyes were rolling back into his head over and over again, and he was incapable of speaking. Jessica began doing energy work with her hands, and I was instructed to place my hands on the boy's abdomen to allow healing energy to create enough insulin so that Dennis would be able to do work on his heart. Jessica told me, "When your hands feel the temperature cool down, the cells have had enough."

My hands stayed on the boy's abdomen and in my thoughts I let the universe know I could use some help on this one. After I felt his skin cool down, that was the signal for Dennis to begin his work. He drew his face close into the boy's body so that he could focus his clairvoyant vision and extended his right index finger over the boy's heart area. Dennis directed light energy from his finger to laser one of the heart valves and form a tighter seal for it. After the work was completed, we let the boy rest and brought his father back into the hall to be with him. Color soon appeared in the boy's face as his circulation improved and his eyes were no longer fluttering. Although the boy was still in a weak condition, he was able to walk out with his father on his own strength. The universe didn't heal the child completely but he was clearly better off than when he came in. We never saw or heard from them again, just as with many others. Not that everyone left in perfect health. Dennis remarked that on some level they had received the exact amount of healing they were willing to accept; that it was a "free will" kind of thing.

A few months into my stay at Mount Shasta, my body was beginning to look rather thin and run down. I was 37 years old at this time, still a vegetarian, and had been holding to that diet for 17 years. I thought it was the best way to live in respect to caring for the animals, my health, and the rest of the planet. It was also a chance to develop incredible willpower. However, my weight was down to about 120 pounds; my cheekbones were becoming hollow and the prisoner-of-war look was setting in.

Dennis, always helpful when he saw someone struggling or not understanding something, came up to me and said quite bluntly, "You look like shit. We are going to have to take you to the hospital soon if you don't drop your judgments on food and change your diet. For you to live, something has to die. You need to start eating meat."

I knew he was right. It was time to listen to my body. Vegetarianism was not working for me any longer. It was time to change my concept of what foods were appropriate for me or suffer serious consequences. Overnight, I gave up a vegetarian lifestyle that had been a major part of my personality. The ease of the change surprised me, though, and I felt relief once I'd made the decision. I was still too sensitive to prepare any raw meat for meals but I was able to eat it after it was cooked. My body accepted it without any negative repercussions. After four months in Mount Shasta, the day came when my finances and I realized it was time for me to return home and continue life with my patient wife. I felt that my assignment at Shasta had ended and so I told Dennis it was time for me to go.

"Do you feel complete about leaving," Dennis asked me the day I left.

"Yes. I would stay longer but I really need to get back home," I replied. "I'll see you at the next workshop."

"Hey, thanks for all your help. And don't forget how much we love you," he said as he gave me a hug.

"I won't forget," I promised and started the long drive north.

Years later I learned that I was there as a back-up to help Dennis on his ranch in case Jessica was going to leave the planet for good. Jessica didn't know whether or not she was going at the time, and neither did I.

The summer of 2001 was coming to an end and Dennis and Jess planned an event at several locations over a two-week period. The itinerary included renting houseboats on Lake Shasta for relaxation, soaking at a hot springs resort for a few days, and traveling to Nevada for some gambling at a casino to practice creating prosperity. One of the affirmations that we were given to use for achieving prosperity was: "I am divine, I am prosperous, I am abundant, and I am loving." We were also taught the trick of always keeping a 100-dollar bill in our wallets and asking it to attract more money to circulate through it. You might want to give that one a try.

In all of the years I had been aware of, none of the people in the Fellowship were ever phoned by Dennis and asked to come to an event or workshop. If we wanted to attend, we just had to make the effort to be there. But this time, a few weeks before one of the events they held that summer, Dennis called each of us personally to let us know that the universe really wanted everyone in the Fellowship to come to this one. Then he called again a few days later with the same message. He didn't know why, but the universe *really* wanted us to make sure we came to this particular workshop. So I went.

The first leg of the event was held on Lake Shasta. We puttered around the lake in two boats with sunshades and did cannonballs off the bathroom roofs into the lake with Jessica's grandchildren. Dennis taught during the day while we were on the boats and at night we barbecued on the boat and slept under the stars.

On our final morning, I woke up early and slipped quietly into the calm water for a swim in the semi-darkness with a few of the other group members. Everything was so peaceful. We pulled the boats up to the dock and walked into the camp store on the way out. There was a television on. The clerk and several other people were watching it in silence. It was the morning of September 11, 2001. While America began to respond to the horrible tragedy that had transpired, I returned home knowing that we had stayed safe because we had received a clear warning from the universe to gather that day at a safe spot.

While events around the world shifted into the post-9/11 era, our group with Dennis continued to focus on our spiritual growth. Each year would bring some form of event with Dennis and Jess. One year when we camped in the woods beside a river for a week, I brought some tennis gear, a net, and a foam ball. I knew that some of the group might be talked into a tennis game. Greg and I scratched out a court in an open area of dirt. It wasn't a full-size court, but it was big enough. The court was partially shaded by some trees around it. We sipped on margaritas and played singles and doubles, taking breaks to inner tube and swim in the nearby river.

Even Dennis joined in on the action. He covered the court well with his big wingspan and made some nice shots even though he had never touched a racket since he was a pre-med student in college. Do you remember at the beginning of this story when I told you I had played tennis with God? Well, this was the instance I was referring to. For you see, before I met him, Dennis had trained for years to experience himself as God. This was the very thing that the yogi Patanjali and the enlightened sages of the past said was possible but not many had attained. The physical body was said to be the vessel that could hold the highest state of divine consciousness and Dennis had successfully pulled it off before I ever started studying with him. Not long before I met him he had been invited to watch when a lady in Mount Shasta made an attempt. When she told the people present to give shoes and clothes to her students in case she didn't make it back, Dennis said he knew she wasn't going to make it back. "You can't have any doubts at all, otherwise you'll fail. She faded out of the physical world and she never came back."

Once you become God, I imagine it would be a hard thing to give up just to be human again.

He said that when the transition occurred for him, he successfully expanded through all the dimensions and became one with the totality. After experiencing that state, he was able to consolidate back into human form and bring back the memory of what he had attained.

Because we were no different than him, he told us, he knew we were also capable of experiencing ourselves as the totality. Of course some of us wondered if that was really possible. Even after Dennis had the experience, it only took minutes for his own mind to almost convince him that the experience was not real. Then out of nowhere, he began receiving phone calls from a few people with impressive spiritual backgrounds that wanted to let him know that what he had just experienced was the real deal and to never forget that.

While on the road before I met them, Dennis and Jessica stopped at a hotel for the evening. Jessica told Dennis that she wasn't able to go any further without more proof from Dennis that an individual could become God, something that he was always teaching. So she stood face-to-face with Dennis and called him on his claim of experiencing himself as the totality, as God. She demanded that he prove it, right there and then. Because she was so clear and firm in her request, he began to repeat the process he was familiar with and became God in her presence. Jessica told us that as the transition began, the energy threw her back against the wall and she couldn't breathe. She described it as reality closing down in front of her like the old black-and-white television screens from the 1950s when they were turned off. Everything in existence collapsed into darkness and then a horizontal line of light appeared. Then the line shrunk into a dark tunnel that her consciousness traveled down until everything became a single point of light, which then disappeared. When that happened, she said, nothing else existed in time and space except themselves as the eternal, omnipresent totality,

God. The physical universe ceased to exist as they expanded beyond it. The ocean had merged with the droplet, so to speak, but they never lost sense of their own individual consciousness. The micro had experienced itself as the macro.

When she finished describing the experience, Dennis told us, "And I'm just an asshole from Cleveland. I'm no better than you. That's how I know you can do it, too. Anything I can do, so can you. There is no greater-than or less-than. Just because I am the teacher and you are the student, doesn't mean I'm better than you."

Then he looked around the room and said, "I know you think you are the only one who is not capable of this, and that all of the others are. You need to raise your self-value."

Dennis had endured a rough childhood with his many surgeries and had never gone away to summer camp like many other kids in America did during their youth. To make up for this, he and Jess created fun spiritual summer events. Many of the organic foods we were served came from Dennis and Jess's small ranch and were beyond excellent. During one wilderness trip, we camped the first night beside a river with one of the guest speakers. He was a sweat lodge leader trained by a local tribe. We set up our tents on the sand and built a nice bonfire at dusk. As we gathered around the fire, the guest speaker asked, "Would anyone like to learn a sacred dance?" Each of us was there for these types of experiences, so we all immediately agreed with enthusiasm.

"Okay, let's form a circle over here. Follow along the best you can so that the beings in the spirit world will appreciate your effort." We stood up and listened closely as he started singing:

> *You put your right hand in,*
> *You put your right hand out;*

He sang the Hokey Pokey song and we busted out laughing, thinking we were going to hear something really profound. We all did the Hokey Pokey a few times before crawling into our tents for the night. This was the trip where Dennis and Jessica led us deep into the wilderness…*really* deep. We had a team of packhorses carry enough gear for a group of us to spend a week in the woods. During that week, we knew that our goal was to communicate back to Mother Earth that as individuals with physical bodies with elements made from her, we had experienced our divine inner nature and were no longer coming from a "less than" sense of self. We were now equal to all things, and so was she.

"These are the real Earth changes," Dennis told us. To communicate our knowingness to the planet, a very naked Dennis found a mud pit near our campsite with some of the most ancient DNA on the earth. One afternoon he brought along other members of the group who stripped down and joined him in the mud. Most of them had recently been drinking tequila and, during their time in the mud, Dennis was able to use the alcohol vapors to float certain molecules he needed from everyone's bodies and mix them with the DNA of the Earth. I went into the mud with a margarita and wallowed for some time. When I got out, I let the mud dry all over my body before I washed it off, as Dennis recommended, feeling pretty good about being able to be a part of the action that would help shift the planet into new realities.

I kept on attending Dennis' workshops and the timing and circumstances always seemed to work out so that I could go. Even though I was under constant financial pressure and could barely afford them when it was time to pay, I never missed one in 13 years. The first time I traveled to the Midwest for a workshop with Dennis was when I flew out to Cleveland. After my consciousness-awakening experience in my college dorm room years ago, I had sworn off chasing spiritual experiences. But now I was in too deep. I had seen too many miracles and paranormal events that could only be attributed to an intelligent, loving, unseen hand of the universe, or whatever you want to call it.

One time during lunch at a Chinese restaurant with Dennis, I noticed sweat started forming on his face and forehead. He mopped himself up with some napkins, but I had never seen this happen to him before except during healing sessions. After lunch, we returned to the hotel and were socializing before the afternoon teaching began. That's when I felt a strange sensation start to come over me. Then, just like what happened to Dennis back at the restaurant, sweat broke out on my forehead. Either he or the universe was doing something and it was affecting both of us. I had to get some napkins and dry myself off. Then I noticed my eyesight shifting; my eyes were not as focused as usual. I was standing up and several people came over to meet me and chat. I noticed that as they spoke to me, I had trouble speaking to them because it felt and looked to me as if I had expanded through them, and them through me. The physical matter of our bodies had become more translucent.

The others at the workshop didn't seem to notice anything unusual. To me, regular life seemed like life on a movie screen where each person appears as an independent self. But I was now seeing everyone as the same unified beam of light coming down from the projector booth *before* we hit the screen, appearing as independent beings. I could see and feel that everyone's energy field extended beyond their bodies as if they were all projections within the same beam of light. But I could not see where the projection was coming from. There was no discernable source but we all existed and moved within it. As my senses became overwhelmed and I was unable to continue conversations, I excused myself and sat down in my seat, hoping the altered state of awareness would soon end; I was not able to interact with people in that state. In this state of being, I was also embarrassed at being so aware of my own personal agenda to communicate in ways that might come off as better than, smarter than, or more spiritually advanced than others.

Later in the afternoon, much to my dismay, the expanded awareness was still there; so I went to my hotel room and went to bed early. If the overload continued for more than two days it would have been difficult to function normally. The next morning I grounded myself by eating some breakfast, and avoided people as much as possible so I wouldn't have to talk or interact with anyone. Thankfully I was able to get through the day better than I thought was going to be possible.

A week later I was settled back into daily life more comfortably, however, I was profoundly changed by the unified state of reality I had just experienced as much as the meditation experiment in my dorm room years ago in college. That underlying reality was always there, but I had not been clear enough to see it to that degree, and certainly not enough to be immersed in it for that length of time. Being in that state of perception allowed me to see myself using some of the very same ego-related behaviors that I thought I was free of. On the outside I was projecting that I was somehow more knowledgeable and spiritual than others. Yes, I'm admitting that I had become a spiritual elitist.

There was a part of me that felt it needed to appear like this, and I could see I was doing it because of my low self-worth. If I was truly equal to all things, there was no reason I should be have been trying to appear "better than." I was actually quite embarrassed to see how often I was doing this, which was basically most of the time.

I ran across a quote from Yogananda that used the analogy of reality being like a movie and that we needed to get back to the projector. That day in Cleveland I felt like I had been sitting too close to the projection booth in a 3-D movie. I didn't share my experience with Dennis, but I think he would have known that I had been overwhelmed by becoming more 'One' with everything than I was ready for. He had explained to us more than once that we use our chakras to project ourselves as light and color to appear how we want to be perceived by the outer world.

"God is man studying the creation of itself. And, man is God studying the creation of itself," he told us.

Immigration stamps from Japan

Dressed in traditional Japanese wedding attire with
my new wife Setsuko in Japan, 1994

Getting in some tennis in Arizona (Credit – Jean Davis)

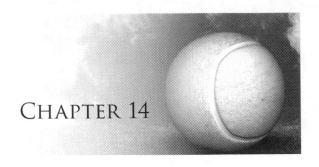

CHAPTER 14

No Malice Intended

Dad was in his late 60s now and had been diagnosed with Parkinson's disease. His wife brought him out to the tennis courts at their club as often as possible to help slow down the progression of the illness. She hoped it might bring a little joy into his life and provide some exercise for his body, which was becoming more rigid. He was fine when he stood still or moved forward on the court, but once his weight shifted backward, he lost his balance and backpedaled until his butt hit the ground or the fence caught him. Needless to say, the scrapes and bruises were adding up. When he no longer had tennis, I knew it would represent a major loss in his life; and that day was coming soon.

Watching boxing matches on his television was about all he had left. When I visited them in Florida, it was clear that Dad still had the desire to be back in the ring, bobbing and weaving and knocking people out. When he watched the fights I could see his arm twitch now and then with the punch he wanted to throw, as if he was in the ring. At dinner one night I pitched the idea to him that he should come out to get a healing from Dennis and it surprised me when he agreed to come out West.

A few weeks later, Dad made all the necessary arrangements and flew out to the Northwest. When I introduced them to each other, Dennis welcomed Dad like an old friend. They walked upstairs to a room in the house in which the session was to be held, and spent an hour together. When they came out smiling and chatting, I could see there was a noticeable improvement in my father's balance and gait.

Although Dad had to fly back home to Florida and continue with his medical treatments, I was really pleased that he had accepted such an unusual effort to help him with his condition.

After hearing that I was again going to visit Dad in Florida in a few months, Mom called me.

"Brian, when you get there, I have something I want you to do."

"Sure, Mom. What is it?" I asked.

"I have only one request: When we were in Africa, I had an elephant tusk. I traded it to a tribal chief for two smaller ones mounted on a wooden pedestal with a brass gong between them. Do you remember the one I mean?"

"Yes, I remember that one."

"When you get to Florida, would you please ask your father for the tusks and bring them back?" she asked. "I would like to have them."

"Yes, I will," I promised.

There was no tennis with Dad on this trip to Florida. The Parkinson's disease had taken almost everything away from him and we didn't even go down to the club to watch any matches. Toward the end of my stay, I let him know that Mom wanted the piece with the tusks back. I reminded him of the story of how she had traded them with the African chief. Dad said he would think about it. The next morning he summoned me over to his recliner. His face darkened over, and all he said was, "Brian, the answer is no." I nodded in acknowledgement. I didn't need to press the issue any further. Even so, I was disappointed in his decision. He had used up all of my mother's hard-earned money living overseas and acting like a big shot; had kept all the beautiful possessions and artwork they acquired over the years; had almost destroyed her spirit and sense of self-worth. Returning the tusks would have been a chance to redeem himself for at least a fraction of some of the unmerciful behavior he had tortured her with.

On my last night in Florida I sat out on the little concrete pad outside Dad's living room enjoying the evening before the mosquitoes chased us in. The phone rang and I heard my father speaking in an agitated way. It was his older sister who was now living in their parents' former house; the one they had grown up in, in Southern Illinois; the house where we had spent many Christmases and holidays together with her. From what I could hear, she was angry that my father was selling the house out from under her. She would now have to find housing assistance and become destitute. My heart sunk even further as I realized my father was betraying all of the values he said he stood for; the ones his parents had embodied and imparted to him. This must have been why he was so full of inner turmoil that he lashed out at anyone who got close enough to spot his flaws.

The next morning at the airport I got my bag out of the car and Dad and I shook hands like we had at so many airports around the world—but at the same time, I promised myself that this would be the last time I would go to see him. When I told Mom of Dad's decision to keep the elephant tusks, she was not surprised.

A few months later several phone messages came from Florida. Dad had suffered a serious fall and had broken his neck. He was in the hospital, paralyzed. The messages said that he was dying and that I should come soon. But I couldn't bring myself to go, and I never called back. In about one week, another message came that he had passed away. Mom and I felt pity for him. We wished that he had been able to enjoy life more and be less bitter and hateful. My brother, Danny, and I didn't talk about Dad or his passing. Jean and I sent flowers on our behalf but none of us made it to his funeral. *Life is hard, Dad. No malice intended.*

After my father made his transition, I attended a five-day retreat with Dennis along with a handful of others. His wife, Jessica, was there, as was the brilliant astrophysicist and consciousness researcher who had worked with Dennis years ago.

During the daily sessions, each of us got to be in the hot seat for a day and received direct input about ourselves from Dennis. As we settled into the first day, he told us, "Don't let this shock you, but all of you are massive control freaks. Massive. This will be our focus for the week and that's why all of you are here. If I'm saying something to someone in particular, and it's not you I'm looking at, pay attention, because it is still about you. There is only One. We're all working on the same material."

Dennis pointed his finger at me and said, "And you, you control people by being quiet."

What could I say? He was totally correct and I agreed, of course, in silence.

He described how each of us tried to control reality and how we were preventing the totality, or God, from giving us a hand.

As we listened to him teach, he would expand his consciousness to pull in more profound insights. As he did, he pulled us deeper into present moment with him. Everyone else had to expand their thoughts and self-worth just to keep up with him as he took us deeper into the experience of "One-ness." Once he had transcended the limits of words, we sat in blissful silence not needing to control anything by talking or asking questions to draw attention to ourselves. After about 30 minutes in that timeless state, we were pulled out of it when somebody needed to return to "normal" reality by saying a few words and creating interactions to maintain our personalities as being real important. The limited personality or ego likes to make sure it still exists and pulls everything back down to itself where it feels alive and has value.

One of the other primary topics we were there to deal with that week was healing our relationships with our fathers. It is understood in some metaphysical and psychological circles that the relationship we have with our physical father is often a reflection of the one we have with God, or whatever we perceive the source of creation to be. Many metaphysical teachings point out that if we can clear up and heal our relationships with our human fathers, living or not, this will heal and strengthen our relationships with everything else we relate to.

During our discussions and exercises we learned that our fathers were present at the workshop, but in the unseen dimension, because they were also working on the same topics. In a private conversation during a break, Dennis advised me that I was holding on to the particular belief that I did not receive enough love from my parents when I was a child. He said to me, "The truth is that the universe always gives you exactly the amount of love you need. Otherwise, the universe would have done something different." He was talking about accepting the perfection of the universe in both its negative and positive attributes as being necessary and equal learning tools. Dennis then pointed out that it was the tough love from my father that had helped me become the person I was, strong enough to handle life and reach for my divinity like I had. Then he said that the anger I held toward my father was keeping me from experiencing more personal growth.

Dennis recommended that I implement the technique of writing Dad a letter using a charcoal pencil. After you write the message, you read the message out loud three times and then burn it. The process uses all the senses and the carbon removes the karma stored in your body that you have with that person. Then he added, "Start doing the Five Rites. They will help reset your chakras to the vitality you had in your teenage years." The Five Rites are yoga-like movements that were developed in Tibet hundreds of years ago and are still practiced by monks who appear quite fit for their advanced ages.

And then when I least expected it, something very odd and special happened. As I was driving back from lunch on the final day of the workshop, Dennis turned to me and said, "I never pass messages from the other side, so this one must be important. Your father said he wants you to know that he is happy with the way you turned out."

That was totally unexpected. Upon hearing these kind words, I felt a deep satisfaction within and smiled. I knew that this was *the* major piece of acceptance I had always been looking for from my father. Years of struggle and trying to prove to him that I was a worthwhile person were lifted away in an instant.

"Thank you," I told Dennis with deep appreciation.

We continued to drive down the winding, country road back to the workshop. Now that I think about it, maybe Dad didn't have much of a choice but to be the person he was. He spent years in the boxing ring, getting punched in the head hundreds of times, over and over by people who were trained to knock the stuffing out of you. That could have inflicted enough damage to his brain and caused his eventual behavior. Regardless of the frustrating and unbearable times our family had with him, we had some excellent ones, too, and that was part of the yin-yang balance we had to deal with, I suppose. As a person, he had good intentions on some level and I am proud of the humanitarian work he provided to many who needed education in the desperate countries we were sent to. His heart was always with the children and people in the most need, the ones who knew life was hard, just like he did when he was young.

Without Dad in my life any longer, Dennis took on the role of surrogate father and our relationship became closer. I think he was doing that for many, if not all of his students. And with Jessica taking on the role of our surrogate mother, we could then dump our parental emotional baggage on the two of them and they neutralized it for us by not judging us for doing so. But even as I was getting into the deep end of the metaphysical swimming pool and felt that I belonged there, I struggled every few months to decide if I was going to attend the next workshop with them. I was still swimming uphill, against the tide that was taking the rest of humanity in another direction.

As we were becoming highly trained in spiritual knowledge, hanging out with Dennis over the course of many years, I got to see the behind-the-scenes life he had and it wasn't always pretty, even for a world-class healer. One year his body started to produce kidney stones at a rapid rate. But even so he continued to travel and teach us, often becoming purple-faced from the agony, fighting to get every last word out. And he taught from 10 in the morning until five in the afternoon, regardless of how bad he felt. He fought through everything to teach us. After suffering through months of increasing pain, he finally went in for surgery. During the operation, damage was done to one of his kidneys and it had to be removed. I called him on the phone a week later to see how things were going.

"Hey Dennis. This is Brian."

He struggled to speak, and his whispering voice told me he was in distress. "How did you know...?"

"How did I know what?" I replied.

"I'm dying."

"I didn't know. I just felt like calling you."

"My body is...leaking inside...from the surgery...I can barely breathe."

He was speaking to me on his cell phone while he was on a flight to Cleveland to teach that weekend. His internal cavities were slowly filling up with fluid.

He struggled to get the words out and said, "I gave Ned...the final... material."

Ned was a close friend and student of Dennis. I couldn't believe I was hearing that Dennis actually thought he was going to die, but I could tell it was going to happen within minutes. I did not want to believe it was going to go down like this. And during our conversation I felt that keeping him on the phone and having him speak even one more word was going to drain his energy even further. He needed to be in touch with God now, not speaking to me, and every second counted.

There was no time to tell him all the things I wanted him to know about how important he was in my life. There was no time to thank him for everything he had done for me and all the things he did to help heal the planet and other people. Emotions washed through me and tears welled up in my eyes.

After a moment of silence I knew it was time to end the call and let him focus on whatever he could do to possibly save himself.

"Dennis, I love you. Goodbye."

"Bye," he said and hung up.

My heart sank in grief and I cried off and on for several days and nights, barely able to believe what had happened and wanting to wish it away like a bad dream.

Dennis had been a father figure to me, an older brother, a dear friend, and such an amazing, generous spiritual teacher. This didn't make any sense. Why would God allow him to die? Dennis was the one we were counting on to make it through the coming transition of the planet. What the hell were we supposed to do now? My thoughts and prayers went out to Jessica and how unbelievably difficult it must be for her now. I felt spoiled having him to ourselves all those years. There was nobody who could replace him, and I didn't want to imagine life without him.

For three days I was more emotionally torn up than I had ever imagined I could be. I didn't say anything about it to anyone but my eyes were red from constant crying and I'm sure people at work noticed. The emotional pain was too great to even bring up the subject if anyone would have asked and I'm glad they didn't. I had to rethink everything now. The glorious future Dennis had told us about had now disappeared and I would soon be without the most influential person in my life.

The next week the phone rang and a person from the Fellowship was on the other line. I knew that call would come and I gathered myself up as much as I could to take the bad news. However, it was not the news I expected to hear. The caller told me that Dennis had landed in Cleveland and emergency care had saved his life. Talk about an emotional roller coaster ride! My spirits were now lifted high into the heavens and I was overjoyed, knowing that he had come so close to the edge and made it back. His health was fragile, but he was alive. *Thank you, God...thank you, God...thank you, God.* Going from the absolute worst day in my life into a state of pure joy and appreciation was an incredible swing. Now things were going to be back on track and the future held incredible possibilities.

Dennis had always told us, "Even if it is written in the Book of Life that it is your time to go and the Angel of Death comes for you, tell it you are not going. If you are clear on your divine nature it will follow your command and leave." Dennis often helped people through the transition of death. He was very familiar with the process and described the Angel of Death as a seductive energy that offers to take all of your worldly problems away if you just go along with it. Its job—and we shouldn't take it personally, he told us—is to find those who are ready to leave this world and help them through that process. If you get entranced by its swaying dance and deeply enter its vortex, there is a point of no return.

On a workshop break with a friend on the left, Dennis Adams
in front, and astrophysicist and consciousness researcher
Elizabeth Rauscher, PhD (Credit – Marie Winter)

CHAPTER 15

Special Times in Mount Shasta

My nephew Dana, and I went to play some table tennis at a public table tennis club one afternoon. Dana played with one of Dad's old paddles, the one I had used in Bogota and Yemen. The rubber on it was nearly petrified and created no spin on the ball whatsoever, but we were just there to bang a few around. We got into a fast rhythm of play, surprisingly close to the ones we had enjoyed years ago. With each rally we moved further away from the table and increased the spin, speed and power of the shots.

After we got further into the groove, I noticed we were hitting the ball in rapid motion, moving our bodies at high speed, and time felt like it slowed down. It felt as if we were energy beings throwing waves of energy back and forth at each other and all of our shots were going in because of the focus we had. It took me back to what I had experienced years before playing in the basement of the dorm at college. The transcendent experience hitting with Dana continued for several minutes. We stopped for a break when we could not sustain the focus that was necessary to stay in the zone. Dana mentioned how extraordinary things felt when we were flowing in a unified field of energy. I confirmed with him that I had felt it, too. It was unmistakable and we both experienced it.

We rested a bit and then decided to return to the table and began hitting the ball faster and faster in an attempt to recreate the experience of being in the flow. But as hard as we tried to get into that zone again it wasn't happening. So I pushed my body even harder. I lunged to the left over and over for some backhand shots. On one particular move, my left hip erupted in excruciating pain and I almost buckled to my knees. I thought I had a high tolerance for pain; but apparently, I had never really known what real pain was all about. This time I really knew. It felt as if a bullet had penetrated my hip and then someone stuck a hot fire poker all the way down the inside of my left leg.

Dana saw me in distress and asked, "What's wrong?"

To keep the pain under control I could only muster two words: "My leg."

I held onto the Ping-Pong table for support, then limped out of the gym with help from Dana, gritting my teeth all the way back to my car.

That night I couldn't sleep due to the pain and tears welled in my eyes.

Something was horribly wrong, but I limped to work the next day and didn't make an appointment to see a doctor. I assumed they would only want me to have surgery. I was not feeling mentally ready for seeing any X-rays that would confirm my worst fear: that my tennis and Ping-Pong glory days were over and that I would be crippled by this injury for the rest of my life.

Restful sleep became almost impossible. Each day I struggled to work and hoped for the best, trying to tough it out just like my old man would have done. But my hip joint had been damaged severely and every time I took a step it was bone grinding on bone.

But I still had my metaphysical pursuits and was not going to give up on those. One of my Seattle friends from the early Fellowship days, Margie Schwarz, was driving as we headed south to Mount Shasta for another weekend with Dennis and Jessica. I was telling her about an article I was reading in the newspaper. "Vang Pao, the general who worked with the U.S. forces years ago during the secret war in Laos, was just charged with plotting to overthrow the Laotian government with a surprise attack in Vientiane."

I still kept in touch with what was going on in the countries we had lived in—the places that had become part of the fabric of my life. Sadly, news from those areas was rarely positive. Ethiopia was a mess after a recent civil war. Somalia had become a hell-hole that we got a view of in the movie *Blackhawk Down*. Warlords were destroying any remaining vestiges of hope for its decent people. Liberia was wracked with corruption and violence. Colombia was struggling heavily with its notorious rebels and drug gangs. Yemen was now unified politically but seemed as desperate as ever in every other aspect. Vietnam was opening up economically but was still very communist. We would never know whatever became of Tekhli, our domestic helper in Ethiopia, of Ahma, our nanny and cook in Somalia, or Inez in Colombia and her little daughter Angela, or any of the others we had known.

The next morning, in a show of total denial of the excruciating pain burning in my hip and leg, I picked up my tennis racket and drove down to the courts at the base of Mt. Shasta. The courts were empty but it was early. Some of the regulars would be showing up soon, and I hoped that someone might ask me to fill in for doubles. Singles was out of the question. I lifted my sore leg slowly out of the car with my hands and limped over to the backboard area. Determined to play tennis one more time, even if it meant this would be the last day I would be able to walk, I stood in front of the green backboard.

I bunted a ball softly at it. The ball came back faster than I was able to position my racket for and rolled past me just outside my reach. Screw it! Mind over matter was not going to work on this injury. I pulled out another ball, willing to go even deeper into misery. After a few of these weak attempts, I was ready to pack it in, and close the curtain on my lifetime of tennis. But I managed to focus and muscle out a few shots. As I began hitting a few better strokes in succession, a white sedan drove by. Then the car turned around and came into the parking lot of the court and the driver pulled it into a parking space in front of the backboard I was hitting on. A gentleman with long, blonde hair got out and walked over to the fence. He looked a little older than me and was in decent shape.

"Hello," he greeted me while entering the court. "When I drove by and saw you hitting against the backboard, you were so intent that I just had to stop and see if I could play some with you. Would you mind? Do you have an extra racket?"

I was almost too embarrassed about my nearly immobile condition to accept his offer, but I had never declined an offer to hit with anyone and wasn't going to start now. It was always my way of giving back to the game and turning people onto themselves and the fun of playing. I shouldn't have said yes to the stranger because singles was going to require actually moving my bad leg and putting intense pressure on my hip, but I pulled out a spare racket and offered it to him.

"Here's one you can use. It needs to be restrung, but it might work."

"Thanks! My son is coming up from college next week, and I want to knock some rust off my game before he gets here."

"Oh, really? Does he beat you?" I asked, thinking of my old rivalry and matches against my father.

"Sometimes. He plays on a college team in Southern California and has a 130-mile-per-hour serve like Andy Roddick, so I need to be ready."

After we hit a few back and forth, I commented, "Your strokes are looking really good. I don't see any rust on your game at all." He paid no attention to my compliment, and as we continued to warm up, we talked.

"What brings you to the area?" he asked me.

"I'm from Seattle, but I attend some workshops down here a few times a year."

"What are they about?" he asked.

That was always a loaded question. "They deal with healing and metaphysics," I threw out to him on a lark.

"Really? How interesting. I used to study with a spiritual teacher in New Mexico for many years and lived in his ashram," he confided.

He told me the name of his teacher and I said, "Yes, I know of him. My teacher, Dennis, did a healing on him and saved his life once. They were brothers in a previous lifetime." I then told him the story behind the story.

"Your game is looking really good. Where have you played?" I asked with enough force to generate a deeper answer. He really had an effortless, beautiful game.

"One year I made it to the quarterfinals of the French Open. That was quite a while ago when I played more often." Then, my new hitting partner told me more about his tennis journey. As a professional player, he had trained with Torbin Ulrich, a top European pro.

"When I practiced with Torbin, he brought only one ball out at a time. We hit with that ball until we wore it out."

"Wow. He's a true Zen tennis player," I responded with admiration. "I saw him play once with Rod Laver and some of the Australian greats." We talked further during a break, and since I was driving north the next day and he needed to visit his girlfriend in Oregon, we made a plan for me to drop him off near Salem (he was going to drive back to California with his girlfriend in her car a few days later).

We continued to hit for as long as my hip would allow. *What a lousy way to go out.* There I was with a former French Open quarterfinalist. If I hadn't been in such a bad way, I'll bet I could have taken a game off him. *Damn. One of these days I'll have to have Dennis work on my hip.* Afterwards we went up to his house and continued our discussion.

On the drive to Oregon the next day, we continued to talk about tennis and our life experiences. I dropped off the tennis pro with his girlfriend, then I stopped to have lunch with Mom and Bob. Mom was in her 80s now and did her best to help Bob in and out of the car to his various appointments. He was completing his memoir at his college writing class and they had both worked on it for years. It was getting harder for her to take Bob around without risking serious injury to both of them, and they began planning to find a retirement home that could provide the necessary assistance.

Mom was always glad to have me visit, even for a brief stop, and I was always just as happy to see her. We had been through so much together over the years, having survived the tormented ways of my father. She was busy making quilts for others, giving friends and family a hand when they needed it. As long as my clothes were reasonably ironed, she was content letting me do whatever I needed in life to be happy.

As for the rest of my family, my sister had undergone some eye surgery that gave her 20-20 vision for a while, but the surgery was losing its effect and even glasses couldn't correct the problem. As a result she was forced to quit playing tennis, which had become her favorite sport.

The next month I called Jean to see how she was doing, and she said regretfully, "I wish I had played more tennis with you and Dad. I never realized how much fun it really is." I wish she had, too. When we had played a few times she was a delight to play with and laughed at her own errant shots. She ended up becoming a decent player after spending a few years in Arizona with husband number two.

One night during a phone conversation, Jean mentioned that our brother, Danny, said he'd had a spiritual experience recently. "Really?" I asked, somewhat surprised. "What did he say?"

"He was kayaking in a cove in Florida and stopped for a few minutes to watch a manatee that had floated up close to him. The manatee stayed close to him and Danny said a feeling of spiritual peace and connection with the animal and the sun and the wind came over him that was quite extraordinary and lasted for some time."

I was touched that he had been so affected by the experience. Danny now sported some tattoos with Eastern spiritual characters and themes. The one on his arm is the Sanskrit phrase *Om Mani Padme Hum*. He also put a blue Krishna on his leg. I'm not sure if Danny knows any Sanskrit, but he likes his tattoos and that's what counts.

My nephew, Dana called one evening to let me know about a tavern near Seattle that has an outdoor Ping-Pong table. I made a point to stop by one day to see if there was anyone playing. I was willing to put up with the chronic hip and leg pain to get some action in. I met one of the off-duty bartenders, and a surfer from California who played some challenging games with me along with a friend of theirs from Spain—it looked like I had found a Ping-Pong crew with whom to sharpen my game and have some fun. If my old man was there we could have given them a good run for their beer money.

***

On the spiritual front, that year I made contact with some people who were fully immersed in that reality. Two people from South America, Mirtha and Guillermo, co-workers in a metaphysical training and teaching center, and a couple from California, Lois and her husband

Allan, planned to spend a few days in Mount Shasta and invited me to meet them there. Lois is a modern mystic and her family had studied with Edna and Guy Ballard since she was nine years old. But Lois was no longer part of the "I Am" group. She had left them years ago to pursue her own path.

That summer I met all of them for the first time in Mount Shasta. We chatted for a bit and then made a plan for the afternoon. I would take the two guests from Chile up to Panther Meadows, a popular hiking area on the mountain. I wanted to take them to the area where Guy Ballard had his encounter with Saint Germain in 1930. We spent some time shopping in town and then I felt the need to get up the mountain before it got too late. Mirtha and Guillermo made their purchases and I hurried us into my car feeling that time was getting short. We drove as far as we could up to the top parking lot on Mount Shasta. The mountain is held sacred by the Native Americans in the area. Some of the metaphysical lore says it is a major energy center, or chakra, of our planet, a place where cosmic energy from the world of spirit spirals down in a vortex into the body of the Earth.

Time was running short before Mirtha and Guillermo and I had to meet Lois, Allan, Dennis, and Jessica for dinner so we hiked briskly over to Panther Meadows. We entered a clearing and took in the beauty. Small streams emerged from a higher elevation and ran downhill, gurgling and bubbling along the way. Wildflowers bloomed in small patches here and there. We wandered along the path and then Mirtha called us over to her.

"Guillermo! Brian!"

She directed us over to some larger rocks beside a few small alpine trees and spoke in her native Spanish. Guillermo filmed her and translated the scene for me later. "In this place that now has only a track—in this place, a profuse spring of water ran. It was exactly in this place that there was a tremendous spring. The stream where Guy Ballard bent down to drink the glass of water has been closed since the 1930s. He was bent down this way to drink from the stream when he felt an electric current. When he turned around, he saw a young man.

He sees the Master (St. Germain) here," Mirtha said as she pointed to the ground in front of her.

"The record of energy is in this place. It is everything. It is here. Can you feel it?"

My ability to sense subtle energies was not as refined as Mirtha's. I could not feel what she was describing.

"My heart is beating too strongly," Mirtha said as she placed her hand over her heart as if to calm it down.

She continued to describe and act out what happened at the spot many years ago as if she were there when it happened.

Mirtha said, "Then Guy Ballard turns and goes toward the Master. And then the Master smiles at him and says, 'Don't you know me?' And he begins to speak to him. Above them, there is a vortex of violet light, rotating. And while rotating, it expands, expands, expands. It is like a gigantic torch that expands from here to everywhere from this place where he (Saint Germain) visibly manifested his physical body.

"There is a tremendous vortex of violet light radiating, and that is also the energy that can be felt. This vortex is sustained by 21 archangels of the Violet Flame, of the Violet Fire. It is a vortex that is always rotating, rotating, rotating, until the Earth ascends. There are 21 higher angels that are sustaining it and it forms a tremendous ring-pass-not, a circle of protection for all of Mount Shasta. That vortex is above us," and she pointed upward and waved her hand in wide circles.

Guillermo later posted the video of that experience on the Internet.

We then stood on one of the foot paths and Mirtha led us in a brief prayer. We sat beside some rocks and she said to me, "You carry a lot of light."

"Thank you," I responded, thinking about all of the training and experiences I had gone through. Humility is not my strong suit.

"It wasn't a compliment," she said, making sure I didn't take it as one.

On the dusty path back to the car, Mirtha turned to me and stated directly and rather commandingly, "You must write a book to share what you know."

I had only known her for a few hours, but could tell this was not her normal conversational tone. The message came through as a gentle but forceful command from the universe.

"I will," I promised before our eyes broke contact.

"But there is something within yourself you must work on," she confided.

I prepared myself for what she had to say next, knowing that she was a highly capable expert in matters of personal and spiritual growth. After a pause I asked, "What is it?"

Mirtha said, "It's too personal. I can't say," and looked away.

Fair enough. I left it at that, not wanting to make her uncomfortable by pressing the issue. I had absolutely no idea what it could be but it would have to wait for some other time, some other place. I had not reached enlightenment and realized that there were still further steps up the ladder of self-realization that I would have to take.

It was obvious to each of us, Guillermo, Mirtha, and me, that even though we were from different parts of the world and had been separated our entire lives until this moment, we had been brought together by having an appreciation of certain spiritual teachings and teachers. Mirtha saw great joy in the beauty of life all around her and was such a delight to spend time with. She laughed frequently and often blurted out what the masters in the unseen dimension were communicating to her.

"Ah, the teacher of Dennis is Morya," she said in English as if the masters had just given her that bit of information.

I nodded in acknowledgment. "He studied with Babaji, and the other Masters when he lived in the woods for many years."

Driving down the mountain to dinner, I reflected on how fortunate it was for all of us to be able to join together. During the meal a conversation ensued about plans for the following day. Lois turned to me and asked, "Brian, would you like to come on a private tour of the 'I Am' temple with us tomorrow? Our friend Janie said that you would be welcome to join us."

"I would love to!" I affirmed without hesitation, knowing this would be a chance to spend more time with them.

"Can you make it over by nine o'clock?" Lois asked. "The owner of the bed and breakfast puts out a very nice spread and there will be plenty to eat."

"That sounds really great. Thank you so much," I responded.

Later that night I went back to my campsite at Lake Siskiyou and got settled in. The campfire soon crackled with life. Smoke from the manzanita wood spiraled up into the darkness and the Milky Way was peeking over my shoulder. The fire continued to entertain me with its hypnotic dance and I remembered the words that Dennis had said very emphatically several times to his students, "To even be an atom on this planet, you won the lottery. Earth is a special place. You have a front row ticket for the greatest show in all of creation. Don't give up your ticket for anything."

Well, tomorrow is going to be another perfect day on planet paradise and no matter how easy or how hard life will be, I am not going to give up my ticket for anything. And I hope you keep yours too. I'll bring an extra paddle for you in case we get a chance to play some Ping-Pong.

To be continued in the sequel,
Ping-Pong with God.

Mirtha and Guillermo spotting the location in Panther Meadows where
St. Germain met Guy Ballard at their legendary encounter in 1930

An unusual cloud over Mt. Shasta

Printed in the United States
by Baker & Taylor Publisher Services